CARL GUSTAV CARUS

SPACE, TIME, AND MAN

FROM

NATURE AND IDEA, OR BECOMING AND ITS LAW

TRANSLATED WITH AN INTRODUCTION
BY
ALEXANDER JACOB

Virtus Editions

CATALOGUING IN PUBLICATION DATA

© Copyright 2025 by Virtus Editions, Adelaide.

Carus, Carl Gustav, and Alexander Jacob. *Space, Time, and Man*. Adelaide: Virtus Editions, 2025.

ISBN: 978-1-7644689-0-9 (softcover).

Set in EB Garamond and Pirata One.

Front cover: C. G. Carus, *Das Großsteingrab Nobbin auf Rügen*.

Website: alexanderjacob1.wordpress.com/virtus-editions.

A catalogue record for this book is available from the National Library of Australia

NATIONAL LIBRARY OF AUSTRALIA

CARL GUSTAV CARUS (1789–1869)

(Portrait by Johann Carl Rößler)

Contents

Introduction

Alexander Jacob

Naturphilosophie, or the natural philosophy that was developed in nineteenth century Germany, was an attempt on the part of philosophers like Friedrich Schelling (1775–1854)[1] and Lorenz Oken (1779–1851) to advance a philosophical understanding of Nature as opposed to the mere scientific study of it.[2]

---

[1]   Hegel too presents a natural philosophical scheme in the *Enzyklopädie der philosophischen Wissenschaften im Grundriss* (1817–1830). But we find in it a completely "logical" attitude toward nature, where the universe is deduced through a series of postulations, negations, and sublimations of logical and mathematical categories. Hegel's definitions of space and time, in the first part of his natural philosophy, the Mechanics, may be cited as an example of this artificial dialectical method:

> Space is the immediate existence of quantity in which everything subsists, even the limit having the form of subsistence; this is the defect of space. Space is this contradiction, to be infected with negation, but in such wise that this negation falls apart into indifferent subsistence. Since space, therefore, is only this inner negation of itself, the self-sublating of its moments is its truth. Now time is precisely the existence of this perpetual self-sublation; in time, therefore, the point has actuality. Difference has stepped out of space; this means that it has ceased to be this indifference, it is for itself in all its unrest, is no longer paralysed. This pure quantity, as self-existent difference, is what is negative in itself, time; it is the negation of the negation, the self-relating negation—the truth of space is time, and thus space becomes time. (Addition, Art.257, tr. A. V. Miller.)

[2]   For a survey of the major natural philosophers, see: Jacob, Alexander. *De Naturae Natura: Idealistic Conceptions of Nature and the Unconscious*. London: Arktos, 2011.

According to Schelling, the primal animate force, or energy, that manifests the universe is the world-soul. The world-soul in Schelling is the innate activity of nature understood as a twofold dynamic process that is the essence of vital movement. This peculiar organizing movement of the world-soul consists of a primary natural force that generates movement forward continuously and a second that restricts it back to its source in circular form. It is because of the second movement that the infinite is made finite and objective, i.e., perceptible as object or phenomenon.

The principle which "supports the continuity of the organic and the inorganic world and knits the whole of nature into a common organism" is identified with the "forming and shaping aether."[3] This aether, or primal light, is the principle of "the universality in unity" and is complemented by gravity, which constitutes a "unity within the universality." The force of gravity is considered to be the manifestation of the Absolute "as infinite and free substance" and is thus the same as the matter that underlies all phenomena.

The movements of material nature are then divided into the three dialectical moments of magnetism, electricity, and chemical processes. The third moment of every level of being is also the beginning of a new level, and thus chemical processes lead naturally into organic ones. In the *Erster Entwurf eines Systems der Naturphilosophie*, Schelling shows more clearly how magnetism, electricity, and chemical processes correspond exactly to sensibility, irritability, and reproductivity in the organic world. The organic realm gradually rises into that of consciousness, which is marked by the three moments of sense perception, understanding, and

---

[3] Schelling, "Von der Weltseele," in *Sämtliche Werke* (Stuttgart: Cotta, 1856–61), II: 569.

finally reason. Reason is "the immediate image of the eternal," just as the inorganic and the organic realms represent the finite and the infinite. Reason, though the third stage in individual things, is, however, essentially the first, and appears last only because the phenomenal world is a mirror image of the ideal.

Schelling's Absolute is thus identical with the ideal universe and has to come to consciousness, just like the latter, through the evolution of nature. It is in its effort to become conscious of itself that the Absolute produces the real world through a continuous process of expansion and contraction. In the process of this self-reflection, it becomes an object for itself. As he says in the *Ideen zu einer Philosophie der Natur*, "For a mind is that which is able, from the original conflict of its self-consciousness, to create an objective world and to give continuance to the product in this conflict itself." Nature is thus an "Odyssey of the Mind" that the latter undertakes in order to attain self-consciousness.

The relationship between the ideal and the real world is one of archetype and ektype. But the archetypal form itself is differentiated into numerous lesser ones. This differentiation is due to the opposition of finite and infinite within the Absolute.[4] The forms, in Schelling's philosophy, are thus principles of "multiplicity" or differentiation, inherent in the form of the Absolute. As such, they are all variable, except for the form of God, whose unity, we may remember, is represented in the manifest cosmos by the universal substance of gravity, or matter.

In *Bruno, oder über das göttliche und natürliche Prinzip der Dinge*, Schelling describes the Absolute as an undifferentiated unity that, however, contains the finite forms of the world *sub*

---

[4]   Schelling, "Bruno" in *Werke* IV: 25ff.

specie aeternitatis, which forms remove themselves from the whole in order to actualize themselves:

> The absolute identity of all things also contains within itself the difference of all forms [of appearance]. Yet, since in the domain of the absolute difference and indifference are indistinguishable, it includes the difference of all things in an indivisible unity with their indifference; thus it contains things in such a way that each thing takes from the absolute its own proper life and ideally goes over into a separated existence. In this way the universe sleeps in an infinitely fruitful womb, as it were, along with the profusion of its shapes and forms, the kingdom of life, and the totality of its developments.[5]

By representing the Ideas of the Absolute as differentiated into infinite and finite, and including all the variable forms of the world, Schelling draws nature up into the Absolute in its primordial intelligible stage, whereas in more transcendental systems of idealism, such as that of the most ancient Indian doctrines of Sānkhya, all forms are products of the Higher Intellect (*Buddhi*), Egoity (*Ahamkāra*), and Lower Intellect (*Manas*) of an ideal macroanthropos (*Purusha*) who employs the illusory power of nature (the "world-soul" of Schelling) to manifest the cosmos.[6] By this subtle distinction, transcendental philosophy clearly dissociates the intelligible realm from the sensible. Schelling's natural philosophy, on the other hand, identifies nature and spirit, matter, and consciousness, so closely that it is indeed transformed into a "Spinozism of physics," as Schelling himself described it in the *Einleitung zu dem Entwurf*.[7]

Lorenz Oken, who was a naturalist, introduced a more

---

5   "Bruno" in *Werke* IV: 258f.
6   See further below.
7   Schelling, *Werke* III: 273.

scientific approach to the philosophical study of nature in his 1808 essays *Ueber das Universum als Fortsetzung des Sinnensystems* and *Erste Ideen zur Theorie des Lichts, der Finsterniss, der Farben und der Wärme*, whereby natural science itself was studied according to the divine laws of nature. Oken also posited the aether as the source of light and heat, just as Carus did in his works. Though it must be acknowledged that even Schelling had, in his *Erster Entwurf eines Systems der Naturphilosophie* (1799), employed—instead of such a mysterious substance as the aether—"matter" itself as a primordial equilibrium of contractive and expansive forces from which light and organisms emerge.

❧

Since the aether is a crucial category that is employed by Carus we may briefly refer to the concept of the aether in the Indian Sānkhya system, which is attributed to the sage Kapila and some of whose philosophical categories are alluded to in the Vedas, Upanishads, and Purānas. Sānkhya may well have been the original form of the ancient Indo-European wisdom, since we note that among the Krita Yuga avatārs of Vishnu listed in the *Bhāgavata Purāna* (I, 3, 162),[8] Kapila (the name of the historical founder of Sānkhya Yoga)

---

[8]   According to *BP* (I, 3), there are twenty-two avatārs of Vishnu, beginning with (Krita Yuga) Chatursana (the four sons of Brahma), the boar Varāha, Nārada, Nara-Nārāyana, Kapila, Dattatreya, Yajna, Rishabha; (Treta Yuga) the fish Matsya, the tortoise Kūrma, Dhanvantari, Mohini, Narasimha, Vāmana, Parashurāma, Vyāsa, Rāma; (Dvāpara Yuga) Balarāma, Krishna; (Kali Yuga) the Buddha, Kalki.
     However, in *BP* (III), Kapila is described as the son of Kardama and his wife Devahūti. According to the *Rāmāyana, Uttarakānda*, 100, Kardama was the same as Manu and king of Bāhlika (Bactria). The son of Kardama is said to be Ila, the founder of the lunar Aila

precedes Yajna (representing Vedic sacrifice), who in turn precedes Rishabha (the name of the historic founder of Jainism). The avatārs of the earliest Krita Yuga are of course cosmic phenomena rather than earthly, but the sequence of these names suggests that Sānkhya-Yoga may indeed have preceded Vedic Brāhmanism, which in turn preceded Jainism.

Sānkhya maintains that, at the beginning of creation, the divine Soul, *Ātman*, presided over an unfathomable chaos. The *Brahmāṇḍa Purāṇa*, for instance, following the Sānkhya doctrines, begins creation thus: "This entire dark world was pervaded by his *Ātman*" (I, i, 3, 12). In the *Bhāgavata Purāna* (II, 5), the instrument of manifestation is called *Māya* (Illusion). The Lord, desirous of creation, arouses out of his own power of illusion *Māya*, aided by Time (*Kāla-Shiva*), the three forms of divine energy that constitute the illusion of Nature, *sattva* (luminosity), *rajas* (activity), and *tamas* (lethargy), in a state of perfect balance. Once this balance is disturbed and one of the energies begins to predominate over the others, the unmanifest deity begins to be gradually manifested. However, unlike in the German philosophies, in the Indian systems the first definable deity—as distinct from the ineffable unmanifest deity—is an ideal *macroanthropos*, *Purusha* (Cosmic Man). This makes clear the correspondence between macrocosm and microcosm that is alluded to so frequently in ancient, as well as modern, philosophical systems. It is the *Purusha* who manifests the cosmos

---

dynasty. The association with Bactria makes it plausible that, whereas the original cosmic phenomenon called Kapila occurred in the Krita Yuga, the historic Kapila reappeared in the Tretā Yuga as the son of the "First Man," Manu Vaivasvata, who was saved from the Flood by a fish (*Matsya*).

that he himself represents ideally, and the agent of manifestation is the power of *Māya* that produces the illusion of Nature.[9]

The first result of the disturbance of the equilibrium of the three divine energies during the earliest moments of the cosmic creation is the higher, discriminating Intellect or Mind[10] (*Buddhi*) called *Mahat* (The Great Entity). This *Mahat-tattva* (= principle) is marked by *Ahamkāra* (Cosmic Egoity).[11] Thus the self-consciousness of the primordial Man lies at the base of the entire manifest cosmos and, consequently, the aim of cosmic creation is not only the harmonious order of the physical universe but also its rise to the universal consciousness (Mind) of *Brahman*. And in this process, all of Nature (*Prakriti*) remains an appearance sustained by the selfness, or egoity (*Ahamkāra*), of an unmanifest deity (*Ātman*) as an ideal Man (*Purusha*).

The universal sāttvic aspect of Ahamkāra produces *Manas* (the lower intellect that receives and processes sensory data). *Buddhi, Ahamkāra,* and *Manas* thus characterize the knowledge, will, and feeling of the ideal *Purusha*. We will find these faculties repeated in Carus as the goals to be striven for by the microcosm of mankind too as truth, goodness, and beauty.

The *Ahamkāra*'s *rājasic* elements (*tanmātras*) combine to produce the *Jñāna-indriyas*, the five sense faculties (hearing, touch, sight, taste, smell) and the five action faculties, the Karma-indriyas (speech, grasping, movement, excretion, procreation).

---

[9]   See, for instance, *Katha Upanishad*. Prakriti (Nature) or *Māya*, which is considered as the power of producing an illusion is the same as Schelling's world-soul.

[10] In Anaxagoras too νοῦς (Nous, Mind), is the organizing principle of the cosmos (see Anaxagoras in Diels & Kranz, *Fragmente der Vorsokratiker*, 59 B12–B17).

[11] Cf. Vāchaspati Mishra's Commentary on Īshvarakrishna, *Sānkhya Kārika*, 3 & 11.

And finally, from the individual *tāmasic tanmātras* arise the five elements that constitute the physical universe, called *Mahābhūtas* (earth, water, fire, air, aether).[12]

The prime matter of the universe thus emerges from the tāmasic aspect of *Ahamkāra*, as *Ākāsha* (Space) and its property Sound.[13] From *Ākāsha* arises *Vāyu* (Wind/Air), with Touch as its specific property—though, as an evolute, it contains also the properties of its preceding category, in this case, Sound. *Vāyu* turns into *Prāna* (Life-breath) in organisms. From *Vāyu* arises *Tejas* (Fire) with its special property, form. From *Tejas* comes *Ambhah* (Water), with taste as its special property, and from Water, finally, *Prithvī* (Earth), with smell as its characteristic.

The primacy of *Ākāsha* is made clear in the *Taittirīya Upanishad* (II, i):

> From this very self [*Ātman*] did aether come into being; from aether, air; from air, fire; from fire, water, from water, the earth; from the earth, organisms.

The *Mandalabrāhmana Upanishad* (IV) enumerates the various forms of *ākāsha* itself:

> There are five, *viz. ākāsha, parākāsha, mahākāsha, sūryākāsha*, and *paramākāsha*. That which is of the nature of darkness, both in and out, is the first *ākasha*. That which has the fire of the deluge, both in and out, is truly *mahākāsha*. That which has the brightness of the sun, both in and out, is *sūryākāsha*. That brightness which is indescribable, all-pervading, and of the nature of unrivalled bliss is *paramākāsha*.

---

[12] See, for example, *Brahmānda Purāna* (III, iv, 4, 37).

[13] See *Bhāgavata Purāna* (II, III).

Of these, the first *Ākāsha* is that of the chaos and *Parākāsha* that of the infinite cosmos, while the others accompany the evolution of the solar system. We note that *Ākāsha* is present even in the chaos ruled by *Ātman*, that is, before the formation of the primordial Cosmic Man.

The *Taittirīya Upanishad* (II, ii–v) continues to name the five "sheaths" (*koshas*) of microcosmic man—the gross body, life-breath, the lower mind (*manas*), the higher mind (*buddhi*), and bliss—that correspond to the macrocosmic *Ākāshas*.

We will see that it is *Ākāsha* that Carus equates with his aether,[14] though he, like the other German natural philosophers, does not distinguish between different forms of the aether. The focus of Indic wisdom is indeed the liberation of the individual from incarnation. Western natural philosophy, on the other hand, is more oriented to the pious conduct of men in society and the state.

❧

The natural philosophy of Carus (1789–1869) is close to that of Schelling, since it includes Being and Becoming in a divine unity. However, Carus was, like Oken, a naturalist and medical doctor as well as a natural philosopher.[15] His published works included several books on zoology, medicine, psychology,[16] and physiology,[17] apart from his major natural philosophical work, *Natur und Idee, oder das Werdende und sein Gesetz* (1861).

---

[14] See below p. 51.

[15] He was, in addition, a gifted painter who studied under the celebrated landscape painter Caspar David Friedrich (1774–1840).

[16] Notably Psyche: *zur Entwicklungsgeschichte der Seele* (1846, 1851).

[17] See, for example, *Physis: Zur Geschichte des leiblichen Lebens* (1851).

ALEXANDER JACOB

Carus makes clear at the outset that all philosophical study must begin with God and that one who is not conscious of the idea of God in himself cannot pretend to philosophize. This consciousness is contained in the individual mind as the conscious mind, as "its willing, feeling, and understanding, for in it we have the concentration of our entire being." God, however, is both Being and Becoming, according to Carus, and it is the latter primarily that he focuses on in his natural philosophical study. Being is understood by Carus as a Unity, not a One. Thus it is combined with Becoming through the aether, which is matter and, according to the Neoplatonists, nothing. For Carus, however, man can attain a knowledge of divinity only through nature, the aether of infinite space.

Indeed, Carus' natural philosophy is focused fundamentally on the concept of the aether, which is derived from Aristotle (*De Caelo* and *Meteorologica*) and the Schellingian system.[18] Aristotle had posited the aether as the fifth element, or quintessence, that is beyond the four elements (earth, water, fire, air) and fills the infinite divine space. It is thus a part of the manifest cosmos.

The aether as space is infinite and, according to Carus, the same as matter: "the eternal original substance of the world—if we call it aether, matter, or extension, or force." This aether is transformed by "the higher and eternal regularity of divine Ideas or divine forms of thought" and represents those Ideas "in a

---

[18] The aether is also discussed in Plato's description of the four "kinds" of elements (earth, water, fire, air) in *Timaeus* 53a, but it is considered as merely the finest form of air: "So likewise of air, there is the most translucent kind which is called by the name of aether, and the most opaque which is mist and darkness, and other species without a name, which are produced by reason of the inequality of the triangles."

manifestation that constantly reshapes itself in ever new ways." This aether is thus marked by vital action as life itself and is in a constant state of metamorphosis:

> Wherever and however we become aware of that which we call new formations, their substance is never to be considered, or to be thought of, as at any time possible as a creation out of nothing but that it must everywhere and at all times be considered only as a transformation, a metamorphosis of one and the same original matter, that is, of the aether.

Carus begins with the most elementary manifestations of the aether in space and time and moves to the disclosure of the idea of Man in the Self. All the chemical elements, physical forms, and forces emerge from the aether and strive to return to it.

The aether is manifest in space as elements and forms. The first elements that emerge from the aether are, according to Carus, the atmosphere and the primordial waters of the earth:

> Everything that we have the right to accept even in telluric and atmospheric Nature as the first forms of the differentiated aether—that is, the atmosphere and the primordial waters of the earth—in which case then only the reciprocal relations (of chemistry) of the individual chemical elements among themselves would remain as the actual object of so-called inorganic chemistry.

Thus inorganic chemistry, "in the natural philosophical sense," would include all merely vegetable or animal matter that does not belong to the realm of organic chemistry. The four elements are, as in the ancients, solid, liquid, gaseous, and fiery.

The bodies that emerge from the aether are formed by the "plastic force," or the force that shapes bodies in three-dimensional form. The elementary plastic force of the universal aether is "that factor of the manifestation of the elements, or that aethereal action of the same, on account of which they are always forced to emerge in some form or, according to the circumstances, under many different forms."

The first, or primordial, form is the simplest of all, the sphere:

> Here the simplest will appear as the most universal and therewith also as the primordial and, if we apply this law first to the difference of bodies, it will immediately become clear that there can be only a single type of body that perfectly corresponds to this requirement and this is the spherical form or globe.

The infinite spatial extension of the aether itself is thus in circular form. The universe is to be compared (as in Neoplatonism) to an endless sphere whose center is everywhere but whose circumference is nowhere. Then, through contraction, the sphere appears as cubes, tetrads, octahedrons, dodecahedrons,[19] and icosahedrons and,[20] through expansion, as egg- or oval forms, double cones, and cylinders. Solids strive for the crystalline forms—tetrahedrons, hexagons, octagons, dodecahedrons, and icosahedrons—while fluids strive for spherical form. These elementary forms, however, denote primitive states of the universe and indicate lower life in general.

Natural phenomena in time are marked by motion; time itself being a measurement of motion. The inner motion of the aether is vital motion, denoting life and directed by the thoughts of the divine Mind:

> Since life in general can never be conceived of other than as rise and decay, action and transformation according to an innate Idea, a thought of God, and since all rise and decay of an aether that has been differentiated, as well as its action and

---

[19]   A shape, or solid, that has twelve plane faces.
[20]   A shape, or solid, with twenty plane faces.

transformation, occurs only according to such an Idea, such a thought of God, it follows therefrom unconditionally and simultaneously that all original motion of such a differentiated aether likewise can never and nowhere be anything but a vital motion.

The first, elementary, movements of life, contraction and expansion, result in gravity and light. Gravity, characterized by diametrical contraction, is essentially a striving toward a centre, originally toward that of the aether itself. In the aether appear several central points that draw masses of ether around them; this is the origin of gravity. When these masses are moved apart, light appears. Gravity also holds the heavenly bodies together. Light and gravity condition all the other processes—magnetic, electrical, and chemical.

Light signifies the emergence of life, since the chaos is dark and the first phenomenon of the cosmos is the light, as related also in the book of Genesis: "And God said, Let there be light; and there was light." Light is related to heat and sound as well. Light is then repeated in electricity, just as gravity is repeated in magnetism:

> Electricity is similar to light insofar as for it too something that has already become something is required for it to become manifest, a body on whose surface alone it develops, either through friction (actual electricity) or through mere contact of two different sorts of bodies (galvanism, contact electricity).

The basic mechanical motions of fall, pressure, and thrust are also dependent on gravity: "the entire wide field of mechanics, with its manifold phenomena of fall, pressure, and thrust, is produced and exists only by the other original phenomenon of the universe, gravity."

The plastic force of the elementary universal aether assumes every form whatsoever, depending on particular conditions of temperature, etc. Higher organic plastic nature, however, gives the elements it uses its own form so that every organic system expresses a definite Idea. The motion of organic bodies, too, is governed by Ideas.

Organic bodies are formed differently by the plastic force than elementary ones. Organic bodies endure through reproduction as similar types or species.

> In this context, therefore, the individual, or organic, plastic force differs very sharply from the elementary, which, as an eternally unchanging formation, permits the change of different conditions and combinations only as consequences of external influences, whereas the former, as the essential condition of its internal operation, establishes a sustained chain of self-destruction and self-reproduction by means of which, indeed, space appears for the first time in order to make fully manifest the individual Idea borne by it in its evolution and revolution—once truly as an individual organic being, but at other times as a chain—again possibly also endless—of similar individuals through the reproduction of the genus, or as a species.

Organic bodies are also marked by the vital motions of innervation, or the development of nerves in an organism, and the motor principle. Innervation is a repetition of the light radiation in the cosmos through the nerves, while the motor principle is a repetition of gravity. Innervation, in particular, is the means of the elevation of mankind to God.

> We are led, then, to further important considerations when we become aware, in the case of innervation, how this last and highest repetition of light, which itself appeared to us as the first aethereal action generated in the absolute aether by divine thought, now also conditions our own thought so thoroughly—a thought not, of course, equal to the original divine thought but still a characteristic thought nevertheless

that is also to be called divine in its sphere, on which everything that is called human knowledge is based.

This innervation of the spirit can occur only when there is a central nervous system in which it can concentrate itself.

> Just as for every concrete representation of universal and absolute light is demanded partly an equipment that concentrates light rays and partly something in which the concentrating light (the focus) may become manifest (thus, for the former the biconvex lens and for the latter some opaque body), our intellectual image too will become manifest only when, first, the possibility was present in a central nervous system of a concentrating innervation and, secondly, when, from the cooperation of a multiplicity of such heightened innervations, an arrangement arises of giving to specific signs inwardly formed by sense impressions the significance of equivalents (words) in which that spiritual original image can be mirrored, as it were, and be embodied in its different modulations—in one word, when a language has been formed.

The language of man is thus a sign of the expressive nature of the divine Idea in him. When formal evolution reaches the level of man, self-consciousness and personality appear. At this level, finally, after the vegetative and animal organism, there appears the spiritual organism. There is a full "innervation" of the spirit,[21] which has arrived "at the self-conscious mirroring of that divine fundamental thought, that is, at the concept of the person ... which was always, and alone can continue to be, the basic condition of the manifestation of the entire organism."

The plastic force that forms bodies is unconscious and reaches full consciousness in the mind of man as feeling, willing, and understanding. The essential connection between the macrocosm

---

[21] Innervation is the growth of nerves in an organism.

and the microcosm allows the enlightened human mind to perceive the spiritualized cosmos as a higher unity of Being and Becoming.

> We perceive then how the thought of that mind, whose emergence is bound completely to the innervation matured in the highest product of the individual plastic force, the brain, totally repeats that highest divine original thought that differentiated, and continuously differentiates, the absolute aether eternally through the positing of light and gravity, in such a way that now precisely in such a polar opposition between light radiation and thought a cycle is completed in which the beginning and final point, God and the mind raised to God, coincide completely in wonderful beauty.

Thus, of the organic bodies manifest on earth, man is the highest, and his superiority is evident in his erect, noble stature, height, skeletal proportions, color, and hair texture. His voice and language, too, are suited to express divine notions and perceptions. Though the plastic force operating in the aether is unconscious, the mind of man emerges from unconsciousness to consciousness through feeling, willing, and understanding. These faculties find their fullest expression in art as the appreciation of beauty, morality as the exercise of goodness, and wisdom as the acquisition of truth.

Mankind always emerges as a multiplicity:

> But though mankind also reveals itself immediately on its appearance as a unity, it is not thinkable otherwise than that it did not appear as a one, that is, as one man, but, analogous to the most specific character of Nature, which is activated everywhere in endless life cells, mankind also emerged, as soon as its moment of manifestation had arrived for it, likewise in a multiplicity and thus, further, according to the universal natural laws, in different places on the earth and, subject to different influences of climate everywhere, once again in different forms (primordial races).

These races are divided by Carus according to the phases of the sun. Thus, the lowest races are the people of the night (*Nachtvölker*, the Negroid), marked by low intellectual development, followed by the eastern twilight races (*Dämmerungsvölker*, the Mongol), marked by a phlegmatic temperament, the daylight races (*Tagvölker*, mainly the Caucasian), marked by higher spiritual development, and the western twilight races (the American Indian), who are characterized by a more brutal ethos.

In his ethnographic study *Über ungleiche Befähigung der verschiedenen Menschheitstämme für höhere geistige Entwicklung* (On the Unequal Capacity of the Different Human Races for Higher Spiritual Development, 1849), Carus elaborated on the differences between the four racial types he identified. The highest culture and state is achieved only by the daylight races, while the nocturnal are marked by undeveloped forms of speech and writing and a lack of impetus toward literature, art, or state formation. The western twilight races have, in the Peruvian Inca and the Mexican Aztec cultures, produced a fairly developed system of astronomy, history, and mythology. But their language was limited, and they fell short of the "goals of higher and truly beautiful and lasting development," which were reserved for the "*Tagvölker*." As for the eastern twilight races, Carus concedes that they have shown evidence of intelligence in the extraordinary artificiality of their script and in the development of literature, astronomy, and art two thousand years before the Europeans. But, in spite of this culture, there is lacking in the Chinese all higher ideas of beauty and truth. Their art lacks the "light of higher beauty" and "a deep reverence before the unconscious godliness of every pure and perfect organic formation, especially of the human," this reverence which we will find in the first radiations of the daylight races in Hindustan expressed in the aversion to all injury to living beings and to their killing, as well as against all enjoyment of meat.[22]

Of the *Tagvölker*, the Hindus represent the quest for Truth in the most perfect degree, while the Egyptians and the Greeks represent the achievement of Beauty and, lastly, the Hebrews Law and, in the religion of Christ, Love. After the coming of Christ, the role of the Hebrews has been considerably diminished by their dispersion and, though there are still individuals among them who are devoted to the search for Beauty and Truth, in general "the degeneration of the race is manifested through a limited mentality and a more general orientation to material gain."

The ultimate innervation of the spirit, wherein it reaches the divine Consciousness itself, is thus absent in the other races. All this gives the daylight races,

> the daylight races the right to consider themselves the flower of mankind, and places on them, at the same time, the obligation, on the one hand, to go before the weaker—in so many respects less favoured—races as a beacon, and, on the other hand, to be close to them and act everywhere as their helpers.[23]

Man can develop spiritually to a high degree only within a state, which men design when they have progressed beyond the individual and the family. The state is held together by Law as the expression of the political life of a nation:

> But wherein is the self-consciousness of political life expressed most purely and unmistakably? Certainly only in the fact that that divine Idea, or prototype of a truly human communal life lying deep in the nature of mankind and of the state, becomes manifest in the mind of individuals—highly capable individuals—and now gradually emerges with ever-increasing

---

[22] *Über ungleiche Befähigung,* Ch. 3.
[23] *Natur und Idee.*

INTRODUCTION

clarity in the form of law. And indeed only a national life
ordered through laws will be that through which the concept of
a people is raised to that of a state.

The determination of state policy should, however, also take into
consideration the unconscious aspect of the people as an ethnos, as
well as the history of the nation itself:

If, therefore, we have to differentiate between self-conscious
political life and a constantly persisting ethnic life within it,
then it will at the same time become clear, as a consequence of
the above, how much the leader of the former has reason to pay
close attention to the latter, and how, indeed, all political life can
be successfully directed only through a proper observation of
the latter.

And again:

If it is indeed, finally, always this unconscious by which the
history of peoples and states is made, on the other hand, it is
history itself—as the present realization of those movements—
that is once again that by which this unconscious increasingly
attains consciousness and whereby, finally, that progress from
world-consciousness to self- and God-consciousness of the
peoples—which provides the true measure of the cultural
level—is chiefly, indeed solely, manifested.

All functions of the state—agriculture and the crafts/arts; military
and justice; trade and technology; and education and religion—
should cooperate with one another for a proper organic
development. External relations with other nations should be
carefully cultivated, since states, like individuals, cannot flourish in
isolation, and Nature too should be viewed as a support to the
activities of the state.

The laws need to be instituted and interpreted by higher
personalities such as princes, senates or constitutional monarchies.

Political life is perfected in the spiritual, and the highest endeavour of man must be his return to God through the innervation of his mind:

> For, just as we generally started from the fact that every philosophy must as certainly always silently presuppose God as every circle necessarily must its centre, so too the entire mode of our observations could only provide us proofs continuously that, in the uranic as well as in the telluric and epitelluric, in formation as well as in movement, eternal divine laws operate everywhere with iron necessity—a necessity that rises to the freedom of self-consciousness only when, in the highest aethereal action, that is, in innervation, a reflection of the divine itself emerges even in the form of mind, a reflection whose own perfection, however, is attained once again only through the fact that it sacrifices its own freedom to the universal laws or, rather, that it recognizes the same as innate in its own being, and that from then onwards it acts only in accord with the same and in this way returns to God in an actual sense.

Natural philosophy, or the study of Becoming—by providing a knowledge of the manifestation of the divinity in the macrocosm and in the microcosm, especially through the phenomena of light, electricity, and innervation—is thus best suited to serve as a preparation for the highest human pursuits of spiritual philosophy and religion.

ॐ

The first chapter of *Natur und Idee* deals with natural phenomena in space as element and form and in time as physical motions, or forces, i.e., light, gravity, magnetism, electricity, and organic vital motions.

The second chapter deals with the specific forms of natural phenomena in the macrocosmic and microcosmic organisms. These organisms are divided into "cosmic" (or heavenly) phenomena, "telluric" (or terrestrial) phenomena, and "epitelluric" (of the different forms of life on the planet) phenomena.

Of the various sections of the second chapter of this work, I present only the first, related to specific natural phenomena in their totality as the universe, and the last, related to the human realm within the epitelluric phenomena that follows the realms of proto-organisms, plants, and animals.

CARL GUSTAV CARUS

NATURE AND IDEA, OR BECOMING AND ITS LAW

Preliminary Concepts

All philosophy has God as a precondition and is only possible under this precondition.

Remark: It has been customary to consider it an essential task of philosophy to demonstrate the existence of God instead of beginning with it and recognizing God straightaway as the original condition of all philosophy. However, as there is no demonstration of this sort possible where the Idea of God itself is not already present in the soul (as little as light can be made to appear to a blind man through any demonstration, or the equation A = A requires further proof), so also it must be considered appropriate in philosophy to start nowhere else than with the original source through which every knowledge of God is conditioned—that is, with the God-consciousness that develops unfailingly from its self-consciousness in every healthy soul during its embodied life. The history of mankind gives on every page an incontrovertible proof of this in that, long before philosophy, the knowledge of God emerged unfailingly in some form among all peoples—according to their lower or higher development—a fact that philosophy cannot evade and that alone will provide it that firm point of departure that the philosophers of all schools have for so long sought in vain. For this reason Goethe too says, "One who wants the highest must want the whole, one who deals with the Mind must deal with Nature, one who speaks of Nature must presuppose the Mind or tacitly take it for granted."

The intellectual principle of all Becoming, that is, God, does not arise in us, therefore, as the result of our knowledge, but the fact that we strive for such knowledge is first conditioned in and outside us by God.

Therefore, only because all philosophy is posited as possible solely through God is it also in a position to lead to God once again, and all desire and striving for the highest knowledge—that is, for wisdom (*philosophia*)—whatever deserves this name, always starts (sometimes with less success, sometimes with more), consciously or unconsciously, from God. So, for example, the statement of Descartes, "I think, therefore I am," points as clearly as that of Oken,[24] "God equals zero," always to one and the same divine basis because only by recognizing myself first as something divine can I think of myself as a thinking being, and only by presupposing zero—that is, the Absolute—as the eternal divine basis from which all Becoming and Being constantly emerge dialectically does it become possible to identify the same with God and to raise it to the basis of all philosophical observation.

If now the divine in us is as certainly the original basis of all philosophy as God is indeed the original basis of the world, it is clear that the raising, heightening, of our inborn divine aspect must be called the first demand of all philosophizing if the latter should achieve any higher result.

Therewith the question first is inescapable: "What is the divine in us?" And the answer to that: "In the broadest sense, everything, for it arose through the will of God." But in the narrower sense, "the conscious mind, in its willing, feeling, and

---

[24]   [Lorenz Oken (1779–1851) was a German naturalist and biologist whose *Grundriss der Naturphilosophie, der Theorie der Sinne, mit der darauf gegründeten Classification der Thiere* (1802) established his reputation as a leading exponent of *Naturphilosophie* in Germany.] [All footnotes in brackets are by the translator.]

understanding," for in it we have the concentration of our entire being.

Having determined this, we should ask further: "What is the real goal of all higher understanding?" and there is no other answer to this than "wisdom." But what could wisdom be other than "willing, feeling, and understanding only according to the Being of God," a demand for the fulfilment of which the first condition is "to grasp as clearly as possible such willing, feeling, and understanding."

But only in God does all unconsciousness emerge from the highest consciousness;[25] in all Becoming, on the other hand, and consequently also in the living–becoming–man, the first is always the unconscious, and only from it (that is, from an unconscious Idea) does consciousness mature through a gradual development. If, therefore, all intellectual knowledge has the task of leading to the knowledge of God, it must—as is revealed in the consciousness matured out of the unconscious—adhere to that developmental process of the mind and, by means of the knowledge of the unconscious, lead up to the knowledge of consciousness.

Just as the basic concept of Becoming, that is, of Nature, is generally given to us for the infinite circle of the Unconscious, so

---

[25]   That is, that which is unconscious to itself, for, for God there is nothing that is unconscious to Himself. This difference is to be noted well, for only to one who understands this correctly can it be fully clear when we speak of the Idea of an unconscious life. For men the Idea of plants—of animals—is an unconscious one (so to speak); indeed, this Idea is even to themselves not conscious in any way, but as a divine Idea it is based in the consciousness of God, a divine thought, and only thence the endless wisdom that is revealed everywhere in the structure of plants, animals, and in the Unconscious in general, despite the fact that this wisdom, that is, the Idea, knows nothing about itself.

we encapsulate in a second basic concept, that is, of the Mind, everything else that encompasses the eternal Being, that is, the absolute divinity, and base on this contrast in the natures of the two the difference between the philosophy of Becoming and the philosophy of Being, or of natural and intellectual philosophy, of the two of which the first is the task of the present observations.

Researching more deeply, it cannot, further, escape us that that contrast of the particularly becoming and the eternal Being recalls once again that between Becoming and Being in general.

Indeed, Becoming includes in itself the concept of all progress, death, and constant renewal and is thereby in itself the eternal symbol of all so-called matter, all apparently real, so that we derive only from it also the concept of the Becoming determined by the eternal Being, that is, of Nature (from *nasci*, that which reproduces itself ever anew). Opposed to Becoming then is that true, that is, eternal Being that thoroughly negates everything transient and is in itself nothing but the law of the universe, which manifests itself in endlessly different forms but in itself remains eternally the same—a Being that, in relation to the conscious mind, assumes the appearance of a certain becoming (just as, according to the above, Becoming assumes the appearance of a certain reality or being) only insofar as it, influenced by Becoming, is always capable of revealing itself only gradually in the consciousness of the individual, as Mind (as opposed to Nature).

Therefore, just as it says in the ancient scriptures that the fear of God (the respect of the divine) is the beginning of wisdom, or, as Plato says, that all philosophy must begin with wonder, so we may declare decidedly at present, after we have proved above the necessity of starting from the unconscious for the development of the Mind, that the live view of those great opposites of Becoming and Being and of the unconscious and consciousness everywhere, and thus also here, remains the most necessary precondition for the entrance into the sanctuary of a genuine philosophy.

To grasp Becoming (i.e., Nature), therefore, in all fluctuating phenomena, and to become increasingly conscious of the eternal Being in all of these fluctuating phenomena, and in this way to succeed in the individual mind in partaking of the radiation of those thoughts of the original Mind, as a result of which alone this universe exists[26]—herein is given the final and highest task of genuine philosophy, and also, here, of the philosophy of Becoming; and therewith it is declared also that a becoming clearly conscious of the difference of those two primordial opposites of Being and Becoming, consciousness and the unconscious, remains everywhere the first demand that must be made of that mind that is impelled by true love of wisdom to further striving on its own.

In all of this it must always and truly be called the first great action of the mind to think of those two great opposites of Becoming and Being, and of Nature and Mind—which we, in experience, never perceive and grasp separately but rather always in an inward unity—here, for the time being, as really separated! Our entire existence is based mostly on the unconscious, and as difficult as it lies from our consciousness to make possible any clear thought of the condition of the living unconscious, so difficult will the thought of a totally pure consciousness never influenced by those

---

[26] In this sense is it that the poet, as a true seer, proclaims the great words:
"But you the genuine sons of the gods,
Enjoy the living, rich beauty.
May Becoming, which works and lives forever,
Embrace you in love's fine limits,
And all that sways in wavering Appearance,
Fix firmly in enduring Ideas" [Goethe, *Faust*, I, "Prologue in Heaven"].

constant fluctuations of the unconscious remain to us; for, naturally, with the complete thought of the latter that which is in itself impossible will be attained, that is, to think of Being in itself as the eternally same, just as, on the other hand, the total immersion in the living unconscious must directly lead to the idea of Becoming in itself as that which is, in eternal succession, different from itself.

If we take all this together, we recognize therefore that it will never be possible for the human mind to master these abstract thoughts constantly and in perfect clarity. But, like a lightning, to attain a sharp view temporarily and to become certain unconditionally of their essence is attainable to us through strong will, and must then also become most consequential for every further division of our philosophical thought.

But now the next consequence of the apprehension of those two original opposites is that thence the secret of the opposition between matter and force, just as that between Nature and Mind, can become fully clear to us—for, just as "Nature," more sharply determined, is nothing but the eternal Becoming thought of as an individuality and determined by Being, and by "spirit" can be understood nothing but the eternal Being likewise thought of as an individuality and, to that extent, determined by Becoming, it is then likewise to be said also that—just as within what we have above determined as becoming matter cannot be anything but that which has, in Becoming, momentarily become—"force" too will remain everywhere only the name for Becoming that reveals itself continuously in that which has become.

But another greater opposition informing everything that falls within the concept of Nature, namely that between space and time, will be able to become perfectly clear from now on in its significance, for it must now immediately be recognized that time is nothing but a constant measurement of Becoming through the concept of that which has become, and space nothing but a constant measurement of that which has become through the concept of Becoming, in such a way indeed that this measurement—thought of as in God himself—determines space and time in themselves and universally, whereas this measurement—thought of as an action of our mind—produces for us the *concept* of space and time.

But, though the preceding definitions from the basic views of the human mind, when developed to any higher clarity and energy, are produced logically and simply, it seems, however, not superfluous to dwell a little longer on the same so that especially the conviction of their essential nature and truth may be established and perfected most deeply in the mind and, consequently, also the progress to further observations may appear everywhere correctly grounded and confirmed. If, therefore, we think through more precisely the essence of the Mind (in order to first complete in ourselves the concept of Mind–Nature in its opposition), the above determination must be confirmed for us so much more in that we recognize that the eternal Ideas—just as they determine the law and harmony of the entire universe or, rather, are themselves these just as they must be called in themselves divine and in God absolute—now, thought of individually, immediately become that which produces for us the concept of an individual mind, a mind that is different from God's Mind only through the fact that, while the latter remains absolute, the former always relative and individual and thereby also continuously influenced by the eternal Becoming of the world.[27] In a quite similar way

---

[27] In order to understand all this correctly one may evoke the complex of all laws that condition the heavenly bodies in their courses, the earthly bodies in their life and being, regulate the formal relations, govern mixture as laws of attraction and repulsion, etc., and one will

emerges immediately and definitely in us also the concept of Becoming in itself, or of Nature, as soon as we think of Becoming no longer as an abstract one but as a concrete, setting everywhere and at every moment a phenomenon that has newly become, and pursue it in this way in endless forms through endless metamorphoses. But that which we may call "our nature" is as different from universal Nature, or Nature in itself, as our mind from the divine Mind, that is, always through its individuality. In this entire way of observation there appears, moreover, the following in a quite illuminating and striking way: in the very many, indeed innumerable, attempts to bring the essence of the Mind and of Nature to perfect clarity of knowledge, there indeed remained a patent gap in not being able to explain how two spheres of such totally heterogeneous constitution as Nature and Mind could nevertheless continuously operate on each other in such a way that even the existence of both is connected just to this reciprocal action. And it is certain that, as soon as one starts by thinking of both in a pure and original difference, one will never understand how an influence of one on the other could be possible! On the other hand, to be sure, it is different where the original unity of both, as the first absolute truth, indeed as the real foundation of all knowledge, preceded everything and was never abandoned, where we rather adhered to the conviction that Being and Becoming are always only different forms of the one and the same original and eternal Being, forms that we, merely for the

---

be convinced that it is indeed all such eternal radiations of a divine thought that partly hold the universe together, partly create the beauty of the cosmos, and that it is just this complex therefore that gradually leads to the concept of a divine Mind, whereas, on the other hand, only an individual deflection of these radiations can become that which is now called the mind of man.

purpose of human knowledge that conceives only in a partial manner, were forced temporarily, and as it were in an artificial manner, to hold separately but that we can never separate really and truly! In this case then the innermost reciprocal action of the two is necessarily understood, and it is forever clear that Nature without Mind is as much a nonsense and impossibility as Mind without Nature.

Perhaps the importance of those conceptual definitions emerges meanwhile in greater clarity when we turn now to that opposition where matter and force are thought of as divisions of one and the same eternal Becoming. But here too it was the ancient misunderstanding of considering the two conceptual forms as originally different and thereby robbing oneself of any understanding of how two so heterogeneous could ever enter into any reciprocal action with each other. That which was called force could never be thought of materially and tangibly enough to adhere to that which was called matter, and matter could in turn never be thought of with such fine qualities that it could have really been penetrated and moved by a fully immaterial phenomenon such as force appeared to be.

Even Kant, in defining matter as "that which moves in space," was forced to introduce here another opposite, that of space and time, and thereby really only designated the appearance of force and did not at all, on the other hand, express that of force in itself. All this is established quite differently when both are recognized as the twofold form of one and the same Becoming. The general ocean of Becoming in which we not only feel ourselves immersed but which infuses us too and conditions us in our manifestation, although we always differentiate our own life (as our true self) from it, becomes through this opposition an internally persisting entity that presents itself under two forms that cannot be perfectly separated, and only in this twofold unity, or something twofold, becomes for us the true ground of all existence in the universe and gives us the deep conviction of how no force can be thought of without matter as little as any matter can without a force, because indeed both are nothing but opposed forms of one and the same Becoming.

But similarly the above conceptual definition of time and space given above will become constantly clearer the more we follow it in individual cases. For example, there emerges clearly here first how much reason we have to consider the concept of time and space as completely subjective, for both arise in us only through "measurement," that is, through an act of our own mind, and we recognize clearly therefrom how thereby both necessarily become something relative so that for us, in the loss of consciousness or in sleep, long periods of time disappear into moments or, vice versa, minutes can stretch into days and years, just as in regard to space a person with a neurological disease sometimes feels himself swelling to the width of a room or, according to his feelings, divides himself into two bodies, etc., and through all this always proves only that every measure of time and space lay in himself just as all opposition of time and space emerged generally only from the eternal inner opposites of Becoming. But this knowledge naturally gains so much more in clarity the more sharply it is followed by analysis, for a Becoming alone—if it did not leave at every moment something that had become by which it is to be measured—would, due to the lack of that object, be conceivable as little under the form of time as a thing that has become—fully superseding in our imagination the concept of any further becoming—could move the self as it were into the centre of an inert matter and grant us any concept of space, and the latter just as little as one can say that the central point of any solid sphere is, for this reason, present there now really as a spatially limited entity.

All concepts of space that we obtain we receive always through a measuring movement, whether it be that of our taste organs or that of our eyes, just as all concept of time arises in us always by pursuing the continuous change (that is, the constant becoming) of something that has become (and in this way also our own self). From all this there emerges, necessarily at the same time, an essentially more precise definition of space and time than that which I gave in the *Organon*,[28] where it was said of space that it is "conditioned by a becoming of an eternal Being appearing momentarily in a contiguous manner," and of time that it is "a thought-form that is produced from Being constantly appearing successively in Becoming." For everything that has become—that is, something definite—is nothing but something determined by that which is eternally being—the Idea—and thereby only a being that has become manifest; and in this sense nothing else is essentially meant by that older definition than by the newer, though the latter has nevertheless the advantage of greater logicality.

But all the opposites that emerge therewith from the original opposite of Being and Becoming, and that have been surveyed up to now, bear the sign and the character of their origin in themselves through the fact that, precisely because they have emerged from something eternal, each of them must in itself be termed eternal. For the eternal as such and in itself can never be manifest—only the divine itself in its own Being and Becoming is eternal—while everything that emerges in immediate further division out of this eternal, on the other hand, must bear the sign of this origin, must have the character of a manifesting eternity—which then is nothing else but to be characterized by "infinity."

---

[28]   *Organon der Erkenntniss der Natur und des Geistes*, Leipzig, 1856, p. 136.

Accordingly, infinity is related to eternity as the world is to God, or Nature to Natural Law, and one recognizes from this sufficiently why Nature itself as well as Mind, matter as well as force, and space as well as time, all must necessarily be thought of, according to their essence, as infinite, whereas each of these moments in itself can no longer claim to fulfil the concept of eternity.

The Task of the Philosophy of Becoming

If the goal of all philosophy were wisdom, and wisdom were nothing but "willing, feeling, and understanding in the sense of God," and if the first condition of wisdom were "the knowledge of such a willing, feeling, and understanding," then it is to be asked now: "What is, first, the goal of the philosophy of Becoming, or of natural philosophy?"

But it has been recognized that only in God does the entire unconscious emerge from consciousness, whereas for us everywhere consciousness first develops from the unconscious. The unconscious itself is, however, only a subjective term for that which objectively we have to acknowledge as "Nature," which then is itself nothing but eternal divine Becoming infused and determined by the eternal divine Being. We may now say, therefore, after all this that: Our conscious being develops only in Nature and through it, but for that reason also the knowledge of Nature in the sense of the divine, or natural philosophy, remains for us always the first step to the knowledge of God in general and, in particular, the knowledge of the divine as well as human mind.

Accordingly, natural philosophy would essentially and in general have the task to apprehend and represent the character of divine Becoming in the unconscious and to follow it up to the development of consciousness.

But the clearer it has become to us according to what laws and what essential life-forms everything unconscious or natural being develops and moves, the deeper we penetrate into the secret of natural life and its genesis in itself, the more logicality we will obtain in our thought, the more we will be ready to apprehend even the laws of spiritual being according to its essence and to apply it to the perfection of our own thought.

Nonetheless there will always remain an essential difference between natural science and natural philosophy; the former has the task of presenting the smallest detail of our knowledge of all natural phenomena in logical order so that thereby we may be in a position to act correctly and appropriately along with those phenomena themselves for the goal of the perfection of human knowledge and existence, whereas the latter rather turns to and strives for the universality of all natural phenomena in order to recognize and demonstrate the actual divinity of the same ever more perfectly. Indeed, as emerged already from the "Preliminary Concepts," all philosophy must be based in God and can only in this way lead to God, and if, therefore, the natural sciences pursue the humanly important matter of the phenomenon of the world in all seriousness, natural philosophy has the task to bring to clearest light the divinity of the same and thereby to facilitate the development of our mind.

Therewith it is to be demanded of all true philosophy of Becoming that it unlock and present the inner connection of the natural whole, the great inner harmony of things, and that in the essence of all organic creation and action it show us the eternal prototype of all artistic creation that is to be produced by free human action, aesthetic as well as political or purely human, and how the last is destined to be manifested partly in family-life, partly in that of a state, so that thereby everywhere man will be led to his higher perfection. A natural philosophy in this sense will thereby also remain the most certain guide for the knowledge of God in itself and therewith to religion in general; for, by demonstrating the secret connection of all life and in God the eternal basis of this connection, it cannot but prepare that elevation in the mind of man and initiate that self-purification that is already recognisable as the highest destiny of our life by the fact that, at all times and among all peoples, it has generated and promoted the need for some form of worship of God, that is, for some religion; and, if therefore natural philosophy has sometimes been presented as hostile to religion, this can be based only on a total misunderstanding, or false forms, on both sides, since, taken in the right and true sense, religion can find no firmer support and a more perfect encouragement than in such a philosophy that, in starting everywhere from God, in every step that it takes forwards must always necessarily approach, and adhere closer to, a true theosophy.

Classification of the Philosophy of Becoming
Since the "presentation of the nature of divine Becoming in the Unconscious" is in general the task of this philosophy, now the observation and investigation of the manifestation of this Becoming generally, and the tracing back of all these manifestations to the divine Ideas that lie everywhere at their base and condition them, becomes necessarily the most important object of the same, and it requires therefore only a correct survey of the sum of all these phenomena in order to derive therefrom how best the subject matter of this philosophy may be divided further.

The first division here, however, is produced quite simply by separating the generality of these phenomena from the specific ones of the same.[29] First, as regards this generality, it will indeed be divided further according to the basic forms of all manifestation, that is, according to whether it is recognizable preferably in space or in time. To that which is manifested in space, or to that which we tend to call the material substrate of all phenomena, belong, partly, the element and, partly, the form. The element, or the material substrate of manifestation, according to the quality of its

---

[29] Aristotle, in the *Physics* (Bk. I, Ch. 1), says something very noteworthy on this: "But our way goes from that which is comprehensible and clear to us to that which is by Nature clearer and more comprehensible. For the same is not comprehensible in itself for us. So, it is necessary to proceed in this way from that which is by Nature unclear but clear to us to that which is by Nature clearer and more comprehensible. Now, first that which is more composed is clear to us; afterwards, the beginnings and principles will become comprehensible from these through division therefrom. So, we must proceed from the universal to the particular. For the whole is more comprehensible for sense-perception; but the universal is a sort of whole, for this universal contains a multiplicity in parts."

mixture, will therefore be pondered once according to the number of the individual elements and secondly according to their genesis, just as the form that determines the quantity of the material substrate will likewise be pondered once according to its number and secondly according to the genesis of the individual forms. Further, as regards the generality of manifestation in time, it includes everything that—as force proper, or as the totality of life, always somehow as a movement of this material substrate— demonstrates the unceasing becoming of this substrate itself, whereby then, once again, quality and quantity are everywhere to be differentiated so that now, in accordance with all this, the totality of the world (in abstraction, however, and without designating thereby any specific reality) can be completely dealt with.

Compared to that generality of manifestation, then, every really specific thing constitutes the most decisive opposite, and there emerge here again two great divisions, since, first, the totality of specific things or the universe and, secondly, the difference of the specific things, and along with it the character of organisms, must come into consideration. Naturally, from this the path is automatically paved to a closer consideration of the chief classes of individual organisms, which then are easily ordered in four divisions, of which the briefest designations would be the cosmic, the telluric, the epitelluric, and, in the last, man, from whose constitution is produced then the transition to the region of consciousness and, therewith, to the philosophy of Mind as the opposite of the philosophy of Nature.

All of the above will now be comfortably repeated and summarized in the following scheme, a short scheme indeed but one that encompasses an infinite and enormous reality!:

Philosophy of Becoming.
The Divine in the Unconscious.

I. Of Nature in general.
  A. In space.
    α) Æther that has become.
    1. The spatially manifest in the elements.
    2. The spatially manifest as form.
  B. In time.
    β) Æther that is becoming.
    1. The temporally manifest as elementary motion (physical forces).
    2. The temporally manifest as the life of individuals (organic forces).

II. Of the specific entities of Nature.
  A. Specific entities in their totality
    The universe.
    (The macrocosm.)
  B. Specific entities in their difference.
    The Individual.
    (The microcosms.)
    1. Organism in general.
    2. The cosmic.
    3. The telluric.
    4. The epitelluric.
    5. Man.

Chapter I. Of Natural Phenomena in General

Just as the general can be grasped everywhere only through an act of our mind that we call abstract, in such a way that of all individual things—to the perception of which only sense-experience leads—only that which is common to many is investigated and involved, so also the following observations completely ignore the processes of any particular living being, that is, of all individual natural phenomena, and take into consideration element and motion purely in themselves, which infuse the universe and condition it as the eternal original foundation.

A. Natural Phenomena in Space

It must first be pointed out here once again that space and time, as well as force and matter, are all only different aspects or phases of one and the same eternal divine Becoming and can never be thought of as something originally separated and having a reality in itself by itself. Only with this precondition is it then permitted, for the purpose of a sharper penetration of phenomena by our mind, to separate those individual aspects temporarily, always retaining, however, and holding on to the total concept of the whole, rather as, in the case of a sphere, we indeed separate the concept of the surface and of the centre and the radii, as well as of the largest and smallest circles, but never grant to these individual concepts a special reality but consider their division only as a means to make the nature of the sphere itself, and in general, more perfectly represented and transparent to our mind.

If therefore we first take the entirety of the phenomenon of space in itself into consideration, then, according to the relation already made clear, the element and form of everything spatial will have to be differentiated, just as they must then immediately be considered separately.

1. The Spatially Manifest as Element

At the base of everything that we call chemical element lies an original and universal world-element that, like everything that is most primordial, can never be perceived by sense-perception but is, and must be, as certainly present as in any given material point the actual or mathematical point, even though even the latter can never be represented in itself. This universal world-element is the aether.

That science cannot dispense with the concept of the aether even if it wishes to free itself of all philosophical logicality is indeed a triumph of natural philosophy. All physicists have recognized that every fine effect of the material element can be understood under the presupposition of an aether, just as the observation of the cosmos necessarily points everywhere to that element that is in itself supra-sensual. We therefore have to make perfectly clear what is to be understood by the term aether.

But, in truth, aether is, for everything that we can call a chemical element and that, as such, affects our senses, as much the invisible and intangible origin and essence as the mathematical point is for every actual one. If we think of the universal eternal Becoming infused with an eternal divine Being, but without the former being determined to any difference by the latter, we designate such a fully undifferentiated Becoming as the primordial substance or, following the most ancient traditions of Indian[30] and Greek[31] philosophy, aether.

One may say that the next requirement (already in Indian philosophy)[32] of thinking of such an original substance is given by the idea of infinite universal space that is inescapably compelling and that at the same time separates all distances—measured, approximating to the smallest parts—of the individual heavenly bodies that are reachable by measurement, as it were, and that cannot simply be thought of as void. But after one was convinced that thereby this cosmic aether became the bearer of all motion, and indeed of every original relation of the heavenly bodies one to another—that is, of the reciprocal effects of light and gravity—and likewise in it alone, as the foundation of all earthly phenomena, the source of similar original relations also between telluric and epitelluric bodies could be sought—that is, the source of heat, electricity, galvanism, magnetism, and innervation[33]—then all doubts were removed that the thought of such an original substance—wherein existence and motion are united in one and the same concept—that is nowhere immediately accessible to our senses but finally conditions all sense-perception itself is completely necessary and must at the same time form the basis of

---

30   The aether (ākāsha, shining, glowing) here fills the universal space and is the bearer of sound and producer of life. See Humboldt's *Kosmos*, Vol. III, pp. 42, 54. [Alexander von Humboldt's *Kosmos. Entwurf einer physischen Weltbeschreibung* was published between 1845 and 1862.]

31   Ἀιθήρ is derived also by the Greeks from αἰθίω (to burn) or ἀεὶ θεῖν (eternally moved).

32   For this reason, the aether is part of the five elements (see Humboldt, *op. cit.*).

33   [Innervation is the growth of nerves in an organism.]

every consideration of individual material elements as well as of all elementary forces.

Now, as regards the relation of the concept of the aether to the individual chemical elements and their forms mentioned now, it cannot be anything but that in which zero finds itself in relation to individual numbers. Just as zero is here lack of differentiation, from which, through differentiations of + and −, the entire endless series of numbers emerges, so the aether is that universally existing, completely undifferentiated entity that, on account of this total lack of differentiation, remains at the same time most easily polarized by the slightest effect—even a thought.

Besides, for one who follows the thought of Spinoza in that for him thought and extension are the final and highest concepts, the latter, extension, coincides precisely with that of the aether, for unconditioned extension, without any limitation, as something that can constantly be conditioned only by some thought (some eternal Being), is for us as little anything else than that which has been determined above to be the aether.

Since therefore we have to consider the entirety of the universe, with all its different substances and in all its different forms, as constant differentiation of the undifferentiated entity of the aether determined by the eternal thought of God, it becomes the next task of natural philosophy to study now more sharply and in detail such a genesis of different materials.

What we encounter here first are the four different qualities in the manifestation of everything that has become materially real, or the conditions of the elements (observed even in antiquity, according to the childishly empirical type of that age, as elements), that is, as fiery, gaseous, liquid, and solid, or rigid,[34] and—just as

---

[34] They were for this reason designated even by the Greeks as gods, as Zeus, Hera, Nestis, and Aidoneus (see [Christian August] Brandis,

there can be no question that these conditions remain the only possible ones for everything elementary of the entire universe in general—so one may declare with equal conviction that even the individual chemical elements are not merely the nature of this planet on which we live but that—just as the laws of number and form must necessarily remain the same for the universe—so also are, to the same degree, not only the laws according to which is produced the mixture and division of elements but likewise also the different elements themselves, even though their individual combinations in every heavenly body will exhibit as many different characteristics as those of all individual organisms on ours. In this way we see, for example, that in the latter relation the plants, animals, and all whose individual principal groups always exhibit many peculiarities according to the constitution of their material associations are indeed differentiated so essentially from one another by this,[35] even though thereby the chemical elements in them can remain essentially the same.

Now, as regards the special elements (in the sense of chemistry), philosophical observation has to first answer the question: "For every earthly sphere that arises, are the individual elements the first thing that separated itself from the universal aether, or are they, in their peculiarity, the last?" Already the law that will occupy us many times in the observation of the history of the individual organism, that "no organic element is made by

---

Handbuch der Geschichte der Griechisch-Römischen Philosophie, I, p. 193).

[35] We have obtained a remarkable evidence for this law through the chemical analysis of small cosmic fragments, that is, through the so-called meteoric stones, which represent completely peculiar combinations, present nowhere on Earth, of known matter but which do not contain any really new matter.

juxtaposition but always by division, that is, by separation," allows the question to be decided definitely in this way, that, in the case of every emergence of such a sort, it is not at all that the individual elements in themselves—that is, for example, oxygen, nitrogen, hydrogen, etc.—emerged first individually out of the aether in such a way that only from these have the general substances—that can in the new chemistry be divided further, that is, as atmospheric air, water, etc.—been put together, but, rather, that, everywhere, the more universal necessarily must be supposed to be the one preceding the particular.

A great and very far-reaching knowledge lies before us here, and as one of the first consequences thereof I wish to first call attention to the fact that, considered in this sense, the basic view of the ancient Indian and Greek philosophers of the four elements does not at all deserve the contempt with which modern chemistry customarily regards it. Indeed, a presentiment of the above law already hovered before those ancients, and they therefore thought that they could call element only that which was really the more original. Just as we are therewith now still justified in calling albumen as a true elementary mass (protein) of the animal body that is not concocted by any art of the chemist from oxygen, nitrogen, carbon, and hydrogen but develops only through vital processes, and acknowledging that always its special chemical elements can be established only through the destruction of the same, so in antiquity water or air and earth were called elements because at that time partly their possible division into special chemical elements was still unknown, partly because one had the notion that even here necessarily the universal must always precede the particular.

According to the present standpoint of science, the concept of the element will now necessarily have to remain for the bodies (approximately sixty) that can no longer be divided, though with the reservation that thereby it be never forgotten that these elements as such can always be called the last naturally or artificially separated remnants of the entirety of Nature, whereas all substance emerging directly from the aether was, and is, and will always be, a universal, a universal that, strictly speaking, is never to be viewed as a "compound" but rather represents one that has the characteristic of allowing again two or more particulars that cannot be further divided to emerge, in such a way that we therefore have to consider each of these universal substances as approaching closer to the nature of the original element (aether) the greater the number of chemically simple elements into which it can possibly be divided.

Further, philosophical observation would never have been in a position to give a clear concept of the manner in which the above-mentioned law—which always demands the emergence of the universal before the particular in the original formation of the entirety of telluric Nature—was satisfied if, partly, the astronomical observations of cosmic masses of shining aethereal nebulae and, partly, the history closer to us of so-called meteoric masses had not operated here in a rather illustrative manner. As regards the former, many researches have—after one succeeded with sharp telescopes in separating around 400 of the approximately 4,000 shining nebula masses of the celestial vault into star clusters[36]—made it doubtful whether even sharper instruments would not be able to finally divide all these nebulae into stars, except that here, philosophically considered, a further improbability is present, and partly the zodiacal light, partly the comets and their tails, are decisive evidences of the existence of such intermediary cosmic substances between the aether as such and already consolidated heavenly bodies. But finally the comet-like nebulous meteors that arrive in the atmosphere of our earth and,

---

[36]   See Alexander von Humboldt, *Kosmos*, III, p. 125.

after their ignition, discharge earthly and metallic masses prove most clearly that indeed necessarily, in processes of the formation of heavenly bodies, that nebulous shining general original mass must be thought of as the first phenomenon that still contains its individual chemical elements in a combined undifferentiated state in the way that the protein of an animal body does its oxygen, hydrogen, nitrogen, and carbon. If therefore, following this, it has become the general opinion of astronomers adhering purely to facts that the rise of a solar system or of an individual heavenly body cannot be thought of but as conditioned by gradual emergence from an aether that becomes increasingly differentiated, the philosophy of Becoming must insist so much more that the original emergence of all special and simple substances should always be supposed as conditioned by the division of a preceding universal and not, vice versa, by the combination of individual elements into a whole.

Hereby we should not allow ourselves to be misled by the fact that in some cases it does indeed occur that a regeneration of the whole becomes possible again through the new unification of its previously divided elements (thus, for example, that of atmospheric air through the mixture of nitrogen and hydrogen gas, or of water through the combustion of hydrogen gas into oxygen gas), for, partly, this is restricted only to the totalities that stand lower in organic dignity and to the binary ones, and, partly, these are processes that then belong not to free Nature but to the artificial act of man and therewith have a narrow scope. All individual organic life—in which we must finally always acknowledge the processes of the universal cosmic only as repetitions (microcosm—repetition of the macrocosm)—on the other hand, makes the above law valid with greater decisiveness, and for all ages therefore will it remain as impossible for chemistry to constitute protein or oil of one of those plantal alkaloids out of

CHAPTER I

its known chemical elements as it will remain impossible to nourish
a living creature with oxygen, nitrogen, hydrogen, and carbon in
their pure chemical condition or, indeed, to fabricate, following
Paracelsian dreams,[37] a living man out of chemical ingredients.

But our philosophy has to speak further now about the nature
and significance of the individual elements.

The essence, the original element, of the aether, however, does
not allow a special description of its existential condition as the true
undifferentiated state of all material phenomenon (matter in
itself), and consequently its actions become possible likewise
always only through its being differentiated in some way. Since we
have, besides, demonstrated above how close and inseparable the
phenomenon of force and matter is in every material existence, it
must necessarily follow therefrom that as soon as we think of the
aether in an absolute sense its condition as well as its movement
cannot at all become manifest as phenomena.

Any material and active manifestation of the aether is
therewith thinkable always only when some definite
differentiation of the same through an opposition of heavenly
bodies and heavenly body systems is given, an opposition that for
us must be supposed from eternity so much the more since
Nothing had existed before it and Nothing can as little be a
restriction of time or of space.[38] But with such an opposition an
absolutely undifferentiated aether is now naturally an
impossibility, even though that which fills the space between these
first differences, on account of its infinite fineness, did not seem
to exist really to our senses. The actions of the same, however,

---

[37] [Paracelsus (1493–1541) presented his method of creating a
homunculus in *De natura rerum* (1537).]

[38] Such a desire for restriction would already linguistically be a
contradiction and impossible.

always emerge necessarily at the same time with that first differentiation because in itself that medium was first given whose being and activity produced a tension that separates as well as joins together those first differentiated masses. It was already said earlier, therefore, that light and gravity (centrifugal and centripetal force) represent the actual original actions of the aether and for that very reason necessarily penetrate and master everything that is to somehow become a reality. But gravity is for us perceptible solely to feeling, as light is to sight; the former acts as a purely straight-line attraction, the other in oscillating straight-line radiations; the first bindings of the entire universe to a unity are thus expressed by these two, and one may therefore say that these two alone also remain the true cosmic actions of the aether, that is, alone pervade all of space, whereas, on closer observation of its individual movements, we will find that all other aethereal actions than magnetism, heat, electricity, galvanism and innervation and the motor element are perceptible only in definite aether that has been differentiated into earthly substances and for that reason then appear also always bound to that which we call chemical elements and the structures arising therefrom.

After we have observed the aether in itself and in its first differentiations, we now turn to the chemically recognizable elements. But, just as in the doctrine of the earthly planet and its parts we differentiate between mineralogy and geology, it would be necessary also, following the above observations, in the history of these elements to always differentiate between a special and general chemistry of elements. The former would investigate in their particularity the conditions and actions of the artificially or naturally separated pure elements that are not further divisible, whereas the latter would have to give the history of the conditions and actions of all those elementary totalities that can indeed be divided into further individual elements but in their character are essentially always different from that of these individual parts and only exceptionally can be reconstructed from the latter.

For all these elements a philosophical observation of Nature has to posit as a great and radical law that, just as the original movements of the originally differentiated aether become possible only through a reciprocal relation between many (light and gravity appear only where heavenly bodies are supposed), so also all special aethereal movement or aethereal action in the chemical elements can emerge only under the condition of the reciprocal relation of these individual elements to one another.

All elements, therefore, the special as well as the general, thought of in total isolation and in an absolute void, would, according to this, be neither heavy nor light or exhibit colours or heat, and show themselves to be neither magnetic nor electric; they would indeed exist as inert entities excluded from the eternal movement of the universe, a condition that for that reason must be termed especially noteworthy and highlighted here in passing because hereby, through the contrast of such inert entities to that which moves in general, the thoughtful researcher is led to the concept of the life of the universe in general as that which—as we will recognize so much more clearly in the observation of the temporal phenomena—owes its full application not merely to the individual living creatures (organisms) but already to all the elements themselves.

But, if natural philosophy had demonstrated earlier that, just as light and gravity are to be recognized as the original actions of the aether, so now, after the last observations, even the concept of these actions themselves should be conceived in a more general manner, and we can immediately declare everything belonging to this in the single important sentence: The original action of the aether is life. That is, the true definition of life in general can and will necessarily be nothing but: Life means rise and decay, action and transformation according to an internal Idea, according to an inborn divine phenomenon, in short, according to a thought of God. But that divine thought that calls forth the heavenly bodies and universal systems out of the aether and assigns elements to them, and to these elements their actions, and determines everywhere their rise and decomposition, their action and transformation, is indeed the same eternal phenomenon, the law, that which is, in this embodiment, and thus also for us, unconscious and only apprehended and conscious in God, that acts in the same way as, in the hatched egg, completely unconscious to the developing creature, the still relatively undifferentiated mass of protein begins to be differentiated when the central points of action and transformation (brain and heart) are established there and streams of corpuscles flow in unceasing circles around these two central points just as, in space, planets and comets do around further rotating suns.

If therefore the philosophy of Becoming has once grasped and established the significant knowledge that the original action of the aether is indeed life, it is obvious that, in the higher sense, henceforth every action of an aether differentiated into some element can be called nothing but vital action, that is, elementary life, whereby it is only to be ensured that, if we consider the aethereal actions of all elements as they are revealed in themselves— in gravity, in light, electricity, etc.—we have to differentiate them everywhere as belonging to a universal life determined by the special vital influences of the individual organisms, as which then the latter are, every time, the expression of a special vital Idea, that is, of the individuality of an organism within the macrocosm, and therefore must be discussed later—when we consider especially natural phenomena in time (motion)—even more particularly.

If we now turn first to the individual elements as chemistry presents them from the finest and lightest (hydrogen) to the most

compact and heaviest (uranium), we see in them a long series—
according to our present knowledge—of simple substances that are
distributed in very different amounts throughout the world
immediately around us, about which, however, it has already been
noted above that natural philosophy has to argue that—even if
possibly on other heavenly bodies similar individual elements are
present that are lacking in ours or in others—their division in
general will necessarily be the same everywhere, for which (as
already noticed) the analysis of the cosmic fragments of the meteor
masses reaching us has provided, even empirically, at least a few
actual proofs.

But now, if, on the one hand, all these elements exhibit the
most diverse relationships to the universal actions of gravity, light,
heat, electricity, and magnetism, on the other hand, they have the
most diverse relationships, attractions, and repulsions among
themselves and operate through the ability of a self-transformation
of that universal natural life that is, according to these
relationships, endlessly diverse, that, as we found above, is attested
through action and transformation, rise and decay, on the basis of
"divine Ideas." One generally knows the doctrine of all these
innumerable transformations that emerge out of myriad
combinations and separations by the name of Chemistry, not
ignoring thereby how many different ways the universal aethereal
actions of light, electricity, etc. can be sometimes called forth,[39]
sometimes modified, and also again suppressed, and if, in recent
times, the science of chemistry has accumulated extraordinarily

---

[39] One of these is the remarkable phenomenon of galvanism through
mere contact of different metals, or the light- and heat-combination
through the mere touching of two elements that are situated, one as
the hardest and the other as the lightest (platinum and hydrogen gas),
on two polar ends of the series of elements.

rich materials on all these relations, it is only to be lamented that one has not yet succeeded in spiritualizing these materials more and in bringing them to a higher unity through a logical application of the genetic method and pure philosophical principles. Hopefully, the near future will succeed in resolving this task; here, at the moment, only an indication of some principles to be observed thereby needs to be given.

But just as it was the discovery of Kepler's laws through which we first became aware that the number and distance of the planets were not arbitrary and accidental but regular and necessary, it would also be our task for those approximately sixty basic elements to first give the proof of the inner necessity of their number and diversity, a proof that would, most securely, have to be derived partly from the right observation of their different relations to the four universal elementary conditions of the differentiated aether (fiery, gaseous, liquid, and solid) and partly from the history of the transformation and division of the aether, from the original and universal to the special indivisible. Only when in this way that multiplicity appears divided into individual groups that are to be necessarily acknowledged, each with further necessary internal separation and differentiation from its characteristic divisions (in the way of our present botanical and zoological systems based on philosophical and genetic principles), would then also their mutual relations, their attraction and repulsion—with all the resulting transformations and new formations—be established as no longer an accidental manifestation but as a necessary fact, and thereby the need to view all these relations as those of a general vital act of the universal elements conditioned by a divine Idea would then be considered as having been truly satisfied.

But, thereby, of special importance for such a philosophical observation would be those elements that we have already called the universal elements, elements that everywhere—but mostly

where we encounter them as products of plantal and animal life—
allow us to recognize the vital significance of their own existence
with great clarity and, on account of this fact, have forced chemists
to establish for them their own division of chemical science under
the name of organic chemistry, except that, in the natural
philosophical sense, merely vegetable or animal matter do not
belong to the realm of such an organic chemistry but only
everything that we have the right to accept even in telluric and
atmospheric Nature as the first forms of the differentiated aether,
that is, the atmosphere and the primordial waters of the earth, in
which case then only the reciprocal relations (of chemistry) of the
individual chemical elements among themselves would remain as
the actual object of so-called inorganic chemistry. Indeed, even the
simplest observation of the healthy human understanding already
recognizes that it would be an absurdity to think that our
atmosphere was put together at some time from measured
quantities of oxygen and nitrogen or the original flood of the earth
was once formed out of enormous chemically combined amounts
of pure hydrogen and oxygen! One will then be led, through a
consideration of the facts known to us from geology, to the
question: "Did the original flood of the earth itself not indeed have
a more universal constitution than the waters of our ocean?," a
constitution from which many other elements than mere hydrogen
and oxygen separated themselves, in that certainly many acids, salts,
soils, and metals[40] separated themselves gradually in the same way

---

[40] Relevant to this are the recent researches conducted in different ways
and published in *Chambers's Edinburgh Journal* on the great silver
content of the ocean ($2^3/_4$ lbs. in an English cubic mile of seawater, or
2,000,000 tons of silver in all the oceans of the world), where,
however, nobody will think of believing that the silver here was first
metallically formed and then dissolved.

sodium chloride is separated even now from seawater?—in which last case, however, nobody would venture to suppose that all salt of the sea was developed only through the dissolution of enormous deposits of salt, since, rather, on the contrary, the formation of the large salt deposits out of evaporated ancient floods is certain. Indeed, if it were at all possible that at one time one of those thousands of meteors that have, since unimaginably ancient times, dropped their meteoric stones or their meteoric iron on our planet in their original form—that is, without ending up in inflammation—approached the earth in such a way that some of its original cosmic mass entered somehow into the realm of scientific research, then the most noteworthy findings would be produced on this and on the significance of what we have called here "universal elements," as well as on the order in which the same—from the original atmosphere and waters up to the egg as the original liquid of the animal realm—should be represented and, indeed, in relation to the genesis of the simple elements, information would be discovered that today remains mostly relegated to the realm of hypotheses.

But there are two factors still that deserve to be highlighted, especially for the philosophical observation of Nature of the elements called universal here, and these are:

1) The characteristics of their active relations in attracting and repelling other substances, or their chemical characteristics in general, compared to the very different characteristics of those special elements that separate themselves from them.

2) The characteristics of their continued reproduction.

As regards the first, it is important because it points to the fact that the characteristics of any universal element cannot in any way be considered as the sum of the addition of special elements that are separated from it, as this is attested partly in the often so great difference of the specific weight of a universal element compared to its final chemical parts, but partly also through the other relations of the universal elements in general to the outside world—that is, through their special chemical affinities and, further, in their relation to light and electricity, etc. One may think here, for example, just of the great difference of the characteristics of water compared to the characteristics of its parts, oxygen and hydrogen; but even greater are these differences in the elementary substances of plantal or animal bodies, where often there enters in addition the fact that these themselves can be of the greatest difference among themselves—in which context one need only think of plant alkaloids and the completely different effect of quinine, strychnine, and morphine on animal life, whereas indeed all these can be classified in the same chemical elements and indeed, with just the slightest differences in the relative amounts of the latter, in the individual substances.

Secondly, as regards the rise and continued reproduction of these universal elements, this question is important not only in itself but also because everything that we call particularly organic life on earth depends on this sort of element for its rise and duration. So if we leave aside for the moment also the research of that which must be called the cosmic rise of atmosphere and water of our planet and investigate only the rise and reproduction of the really organic universal elements—indeed, the most important of these, the egg—we encounter immediately the noteworthy phenomenon that we see it, and everything similar, divided always, and in enormous relations of mass, into its individual chemical elements, but it is never a new beginning of the same, an immediate renewed pristine emergence out of its chemical elements; we are always aware of only a further development of the same as something already present, of course, under the condition of a derivation of ever newer chemical elements, even though we have no concept of how an egg is to be constituted in itself out of its chemical elements or develops in reality.

Further, a certain gradation of universal elementary vital substance for different stages of organic life emerges clearly here, for we see, indeed, the lower organisms of simple plants reproducing their vegetable egg-white—whose primary emergence or original production always lies outside the sphere of our experience—by its constant division directly out of the chemical elements of air and water and earth, whereas, on the other hand, animal life is capable—and indeed the more highly organized it is— only of substituting its egg-white and reproducing itself from the already prepared organic egg-white of other animals or plants, and absorbs individual chemical elements only here and there in order to promote somehow in this way the endless reproduction of its own and universal elements. Thus, therefore, just as all knowledge, even of the experienced chemist, remains quite incapable of constituting even a drop of new egg-white, and egg-white develops everywhere only out of another given egg-white, this endless chain also points, in the final analysis, to a secret first beginning of which we lack all knowledge. Philosophical observation would now be justified to a certain degree in this context in demanding of exact science at least approximate calculations of the quantity of ovarian material as such on earth, apart from all the individual organic beings whose chief substance is formed out of it—and this indeed in order to decide the question whether, in the constant destruction occurring in a thousand ways of this universal element, that is, in the constant division of the same into its chemical elements, both during the life and during the decay of earthly organisms, the absolute quantity of egg-white in total—through its continued organic new formation—will increase, remain unchanged, or decrease. Of course, this is a question that demands something impossible, which, however, we do not fail to pose because, in itself, it turns its attention to those secret processes of a really characteristic continuous creation not only of individuals but also of matter, the constant observation of which doubtless leads most certainly to recognizing with great clarity that not only for the world of forms but also for that of mixtures it is true, if we acknowledge as the primordial phenomenon of every manifestation and as the highest law of formation in general, that wherever and however we become aware of that which we call new formations, their substance is never to be considered, or to be thought of, as at any time possible as a creation out of nothing, but that it must everywhere and at all times be considered only as a transformation, a metamorphosis of one and the same original matter, that is, of the aether.

If therefore, from this standpoint, we cast a glance again at the endless ocean of a matter that serves everywhere as the basis of innumerable beings in eternal transformations, we become aware:

1. That in this world of elements, just as in that of forms, everywhere there rules as the first law: the striving from the universal to the particular, that is, we see that, where any formation arises originally, that which we have called the universal element always emerges first (whether this is in the formation of a meteoric ball, and apparently of every heavenly body, or in that of a plant or an animal), and recognize that, just as the sharp division of form is always only the last in the becoming of every organism, so also the pure chemical element is always either the last in the free development of matter or—indeed, in most cases—is represented as such only by the deliberate divisions of human chemical analysis.

2. The opposed formative directions from a particular matter to the universal will always be possible only under two

conditions, that is, either by virtue of the fact that an already present universal element gathers the elements that have the same name as the individual chemical elements contained in it from other combinations or also those existing in themselves, and, by means of the aethereal action that we call the individual plastic force, develops its own mass through these elements (this is the way, for example, that an ovarian material in all organisms renews itself constantly); or else by virtue of the fact that, either accidentally or deliberately, individual pure chemical elements are united and, through the stimulation of some other aethereal action, are transformed into a more universal element. One of these processes—which moreover is present only occasionally and in secondary cases— will be when, for example, oxygen and hydrogen are joined again in this way to water through electric sparks (in which case, however, it is to be noted that generally in the case of all chemical divisions and combinations an electric process takes place that is sometimes visible and at other times invisible).

3. Finally, there exists between universal and chemical elements another immeasurable multiplicity of individual intermediate substances that have arisen either through the organic division of the former or through chemical and mechanical combination of the latter, in which, through reciprocal exchange of the constituents and ever-new combinations and divisions, endless metamorphoses in endlessly different relations and forms proceed in an uninterrupted way, and thereby complete on our planet the image of that telluric life of matter which the philosophy of Becoming had the task of adumbrating in some principal traits, and here at least its most essential ones. Such intermediate substances as arise partly through individual organic life (for example, resin, fats, oils, sugars, etc.), or are

formed in the elementary life of plants (for example, sulphuric metals, salts, mineral sources, etc.), or, finally, are produced artificially (for example, the artificial alloys, enamels, tinctures, etc.), are those out of whose enormous multiplicity man has, for individual life goals, learnt to invent the most important alleviations and advancements of his existence, but which will remain only of subordinate significance for the task to be discussed here.

Before we close the observation of the world of elements here completely, another question cannot be avoided which, since it can never be answered by exact scientific research, must here be discussed in its philosophical significance, and this is: "Does it occur in the sphere of a heavenly body created at some time, such as that of our earth, that masses of elements return once again into the condition of the least differentiated aether (such as it is to be considered when filling endless space), that is, that they fully disappear from the sphere of that which can be apprehended by us and that, on the other hand, other masses emerge as new differentiations out of this aether? or is this constant formation of it backwards and forwards to be thought of as fully completed in itself since the first emergence of every such cosmic sphere?"

The question is indeed very important but also very difficult and, if it were not so closely related to the question of either the sexual reproduction of individuals or of their possible emergence through *generatio aequivoca*[41] that it receives therefrom much illumination, it would be less possible to think of an answer to it. In any case, one can maintain that, if our entire telluric organism were something completely isolated and existing by itself, it should be declared immediately and decisively that even the entire mass of

---

[41]   [Spontaneous generation, an obsolete theory that maintained that living creatures could arise from nonliving matter.]

fine elements would remain one that is always inalterably like itself, existing in an unceasing change among these elements, but finally neither really destroying itself partly nor really reestablishing itself partly. But since such an unconditional state of isolation does not at all occur and, rather more, the relation of the earth to the solar system is an incessantly continuing one and the entry of the same into ever new regions of the universal space is an incontrovertible fact, all those possibilities can hardly be cut off briefly and apodictically, and indeed, through the periodic entry of the meteors that appear like cosmic infusoria, as it were, into the planetary mass, a partial increase in mass, on a small scale at least, is also really evidenced. In spite of this, nevertheless that partial dissolution of earthly substances into aether that is here questioned—and the new formation of other substances out of the aether—is in no way demonstrated and, since the observation of the world of epitelluric organisms and their history indeed allows one to clearly recognize how here the rise of unconditionally new forms was always solely tied to certain major periods of the creation of which we can definitely demonstrate three or four consecutive ones in the stratification of the layers of the earth according to their sediments whereas at present such new formations in general are absent and now appear only here and there in the deepest regions of life, all this argues that, even with regard to matter, a partial decay into aether and new emergence out of aether has repeated itself on the whole only after similar periods, or perhaps even those of the same name, whereas such processes outside these periods are either entirely lacking (which can hardly be supposed) or may be limited to just the edges of the atmosphere and its reciprocal effect on the aether of space. That there is in the latter factor the indeed surprising constancy and immutability of atmosphere and waters together, both of which—despite the enormous continuous consumption of individual parts and the no less continuous mixture of foreign matter—constantly maintain themselves at the same level of mixture is difficult to be satisfactorily explained in any other way. In the latter context, one recalls, for example, the results of so many eudiometric tests of the atmospheric air in the most diverse heights and in the most diverse locations, often polluted by all sorts of effluvia, that constantly showed equal proportions of the separated nitrogen and oxygen and thinks at the same time of the enormous consumption of oxygen in every minute and therewith of the constant degeneration of one part of the air. Similarly, the waters always reestablish their original nature after myriad pollutions and once again, for the most part, only by means of their constant circulation through the atmosphere as effluvia and sediments, and whether even there in these enormous proportions of mass (one may think, for example, just of the effluvia of the ocean in the course of a single rotation of the earth) actual degeneration and new formation into and out of the aether do not occur at the same time and thereby contribute to maintaining the constancy of the generally fluid element is at least a not improbable presupposition and would to that extent contribute to throwing some light on the answer to the question posed above.

But, just as in the above our observation had at first turned towards the universal of natural phenomena insofar as we encounter it as elementary matter—and this indeed considered in itself and, therefore, formless—now it has the task to direct itself (and that fully excluding the quality of the mixture) towards the form alone, that is, towards the universal of the thousand-fold diversity of shapes in which everything that is called matter appears to us and in which alone it can appear to us.

2. The Spatially Manifest as Form

a. Form in itself (ideal form)

In all that we call form, we distinguish four elements, of which one includes in itself the universal, the other three as special ones: they are body, surface, line, point. Normally, the relations of these factors are represented in such a way that one takes the point as the original, which allows the line to form in points that move in filling space; one thinks of the surface arising out of this movement filling space, and from the latter one finally constructs a body in a similar fashion. But such an idea is completely unphilosophical and as illogical as if one wished to put together our bodies out of individual muscles, nerves, and bones; it is indeed so much the more erroneous since it presupposes an impossibility in the real sense. For a point, in its mathematical character, is a nothing; it does not fill space and can therefore as little form a line in space through its movement as the latter can form, through its lateral movement, a surface, and consequently also no body. Accordingly, even here, we see that we are again bound to the great law of all genesis that prescribes the path from the universal to the particular as the only organic one and according to which we had, even in the above, to investigate the division of the elements, that is, of matter.

Therefore, the true and universal elementary or basic condition of all form is always one: that is, body, for only in it are all three dimensions of space—length, breadth, depth—demonstrable at the same time. But through the observation of the character of body and the differentiation of its divisions, we first arrive at the particular form-elements and declare from this standpoint: all limitation of a body occurs only through the surface, all limitation of a surface only through the line, and all limitation of a line only through the point.

The deep philosophical aspect of these relations will emerge so much more when we think of the fact that, in every true organic whole, every separation of parts means killing the parts, in that such a separated piece can no longer be capable of an independent existence, and it would itself have to directly become a whole. If we apply this, therefore, to the investigation of the nature of a body in itself, we find always that, in accordance with the above, now also here its individual constituents—surface, line, point—no longer have any true reality in space but always remain purely ideal or imaginary, since that is lacking to each of them by which existence in space must be characterized, that is, the demonstrability of all three dimensions at the same time. But if we have thereby established now the elements of everything corporeal in space in general, philosophical observation has to go further and demonstrate in detail also the genesis of the different possible particular forms of all these elements. Even here the simplest will appear as the most universal and therewith also as the primordial, and if we apply this law first to the difference of bodies, it will immediately become clear that there can be only a single type of body that perfectly corresponds to this requirement, and this is the spherical form or globe. It is only this form in which all radii and all diameters are perfectly equal, and the superficies includes, with the smallest extension, the greatest space, since it is bent in a uniform way in all directions, so that then, therefore, also every fluid or half-fluid mass, as soon as it is left all alone—undisturbed from the outside—to its tendency to its inner centre, must always necessarily represent itself precisely in this original and simplest of all forms. The globe is at the same time the body that, of the three special form-elements (surface, line, point), allows only surface and the point to be differentiated (as superficies and central point) but in itself does not yet anywhere represent the line, because, in fact, there exists no limitation of surface, so that here the line emerges—

and indeed only as the axis of the globe—only when the last of its original motions, rotation, begins, a motion whose further significance can be spoken of only through a study of motions.

The globe is therewith really the true zero of the world of forms, and just as, in arithmetic, out of it the numerical series first emerges through the opposition of positive and negative magnitudes, so there develop directly out of the simplest and therefore most primitive form of the sphere two series of bodies: the first through increased and diverse forms of contraction, the other through increased and diverse forms of extension.

In both directions, the most noteworthy laws are valid. As regards contraction, the three dimensions (breadth, height, depth) will generally become valid as the characteristic of every body, and since therewith—according to three diameters intersecting themselves at right angles, and in each according to two semi-diameters at opposite poles—the attraction towards the centre flattens the spherical surface by six points, there emerges the first angular form, the cube, the hexahedron. Not less important for such an attraction towards the centre is the tetrad, since every spherical surface, containing precisely four times the surface of one of its largest circles, must already thereby receive the disposition to a quadrifurcation and crystallization with four surfaces, whereby then the simple three-sided pyramid, the tetrahedron, emerges. There follows thus this series: eight, twelve, and twenty, and the consequences of these are the octahedron, dodecahedron, and icosahedron, wherewith the number of the bodies that are alone possible according to the rules (a knowledge that had already emerged among the Greeks, and thus these five are also called "Platonic bodies"[42]) is fully closed.

---

[42] [Platonic solids are regular polyhedra, of which there are five forms: tetrahedron (four faces), cube (six faces), octahedron (eight faces),

But as regards the forms that develop through extension out of the sphere, it begins with the egg form, which then, through total disintegration of the entire sphere from its centre, is followed by the double cone, from which finally, by the reestablished unity of the two cones, or their merging, is produced the cylinder. Then, through modifications and combinations of all these basic shapes, there arise all the other regular ones, but in this way there arise also, finally, through ever-increasing deviation from the regular limits, the endless number of irregular bodies.

After we have thus cast a glance at the world of forms generally, we must first point to what a deep secret connection exists between the difference of form and the difference of elements, as well as the different conditions of the latter. But we had discovered that everything that is called element is represented either as a fluid (watery or gaseous), solid, or fiery, and the first thing that we have to add to this knowledge further is that each of these types of phenomena always has at the same time a definite relation to definite forms. First, everything fluid strives necessarily, following its nature, for a spherical form, and where we find a fluid we always find it as an independent globe (when it is free) or as a part of a globe (when it is not free and partially included). That every fluid thing, either as a watery fluid or floating as vapour in the air, assumes a spherical shape is well known, but that every surface of a fluid, whether it be the water in a bowl or in a pond, like the water

---

dodecahedron (twelve faces), and icosahedron (twenty faces). Plato discusses these solids in *Timaeus*, 53b2. He associated these solids with the elements: earth with the cube, air with the octahedron, water with the icosahedron, and fire with the tetrahedron. The fifth element, which he called "heaven," was associated by him with the dodecahedron, and Aristotle later (*De Caelo*) considered heaven to be constituted of the aether.]

in an ocean, always forms a part of a spherical surface is less easy to imagine[43] and is often less thought of, but is the necessary consequence of its general relation to the spherical shape of the earth. Gas too behaves in a similar way, and just as the atmospheric air, sometimes denser, sometimes less dense, lies as a perfect hollow sphere around the solid body of the earth and its waters, so also, in an absolutely empty space and without any relation to any heavenly body, a portion of air, as well as water in the air, can be thought of only in a spherical form, just as a luminiferous aether[44] massed together in a spherical shape always tends to be thought of as the first manifestation of the heavenly bodies and, at the same stage, represents itself actually also in comets and meteors.

Contrary to fluids, solids—when, through their own inner striving, they assume a shape—as a contracted and thereby thickened mass of an original sphere, as it were, always strive first for the five original forms of crystals: the tetrahedron, the hexahedron, the octahedron, dodecahedron, icosahedron, as the forms (that, to be sure, are never present in nature in an absolute mathematical purity) from which, through partial modification, then all the other crystal forms can be developed. On the other hand, everywhere that solids are deposited mechanically from fluids and freely solidify as the basis of these fluids in a crystalline or non-crystalline form, the spherical form will also necessarily be

---

[43] The difference of a perfectly straight line and that of an arc segment of the earthly globe is naturally not perceptible to our senses in such a small dimension, but certainly exists in itself and also in this very small space.

[44] [The luminiferous aether was postulated by some scientists, from the seventeenth to the middle of the nineteenth century, as a medium for the propagation of light.]

striven for again, which is the way in which the firm hollow-spherical shell of the planet itself had to be formed once.

Accordingly, just as fluids or solids are characterized by spherical concentration as drops or Platonic bodies, fire is characterized by straight-line forms of the cone and double cone emergent from the sphere through extension, for the cone is always the original form of a flame, and everywhere the illumination of a glowing point is regulated according to its type of all-sided radiation as double cones.

If, in general, the original relations of certain conditions of the elements to certain species of the world of forms have now been determined, it must still be indicated specifically how manifold the relations are, at the same time, that present themselves between individual modifications of the above-mentioned original forms and the universal as well as special elements according to their chemical quality. It could provide rich materials here for a far-reaching study not only to describe all those individual elements according to their characteristic formal relations that they present at any time to observation, but also to discover at the same time these relations according to their inner symbolic significance. A general survey of the philosophy of Becoming, such as the present one, can, however, in the case of such tasks, dwell only on the broadest outlines, and so let us think here a little more in detail of a universal or original element of our planet—of water and its different forms, for example. But that everything that was already said earlier, in general, of the fluid condition is particularly true of it as watery fluid is obvious; on the other hand, its formal relations emerge so much more characteristically when the same element is represented in its striving for solidification of the phenomenon, that is, in freezing, as ice.

The significance of water (in that it appears here at the same time essentially as the original element of everything organic on earth) is very definitely recognizable, on the one hand, already through the development of all its crystalline forms from the simple original form of solids, that is, from the tetrahedron, and, on the other hand, through the enormous multiplicity in the accumulations of these crystalline forms and in the definite inclination of all these masses out of the merely absolutely mathematical towards the individual plastic force of these organic forms. Indeed, as regards the original in these crystalline forms, insofar as they emerge from the tetrahedron, its emergence is justified by the fact that the body limited by four isosceles triangles is indeed the simplest, and therewith is the primordial one, and all ice crystals therefore are based—according to their development— on a triad and its doubling into a hexad, for which then the enormous multiplicity of forms of snowflakes provide the best commentaries. On the other hand, as regards the transition of the accumulated geometric original forms into organic ones, one may notice just the crystalline forms of ice, such as are represented in so many ways in window ice, in that they—even though individually traceable to three-sided spicules and flakes—still show tendencies that cannot but be designated as presentiments of characteristic individual vital phenomena, and to which we shall return as soon as those individual vital phenomena are to be considered.[45]

---

[45]   It is highly noteworthy how this tendency of solidifying water also sweeps along—and every time in a characteristic manner— substances mixed with it in the solution towards these individually organic forms. Thereby are explained not only the remarkably shooting forms of crystallizing metallic salts (like a fir tree), but also how even metallic solutions dropped on blotting paper produce the most delicate coloured images, which again repeat the colour patterns of flowers and molluscs. On this, F. F. Runge (*Der Bildungstrieb der Stoffe, veranschaulicht in selbstständig gewachsenen Bildern,*

But let us leave now all crystalline phenomena and return to the original form of the sphere, of which natural philosophical observation still has to highlight other extremely noteworthy characteristics, among which the most important may be mentioned: that stereometry[46] can provide proof of the fact that "the surface of a sphere is always exactly equal to the fourfold surface space of a large circle of the same," wherewith it is then also directly given that in every peripheral surface of a sphere is contained the disposition to a pure quadrifurcation, just as, again, every circle has the disposition to a sexpartition through the fact that the radius of the circle is itself exactly equal to a side of the hexagon within this circle. But these great mathematical laws of form are important to natural philosophy because they now actually operate and are realized in thousands of phenomena of natural life, phenomena that—so long as we do not understand this deeper basis—cannot but appear to us always as wonderful, but which, explained to us by this key, are immediately explicable as conditioned by inner necessity. Already the immediate emergence of the difference between meridian and equator in every sphere—as soon as it is set in motion and thereby an axis and two poles are posited in it, from which then proceeds also the old necessity of dividing the earth and heaven according to meridian and equator and thereafter the original division of a light meeting the spherical surface in the form of a cross—which is manifest so clearly in every halo around the sun and moon (through the four

---

Oranienburg, 1855) has given us a very interesting work that has been noted much less than it deserves.

46   [Stereometry is the measurement of solid bodies.]

light spots conditioning the so-called parhelia[47])—and finally the quadrifurcation everywhere in higher organisms repeated in the four bodily aspects, and already manifest in the first cleavage of the developing egg in the case of most animals—all these and so many other phenomena are always explained and conditioned only by that great law. If one now takes, in addition, the similarly endlessly repeating division of the circle according to a hexad, such as emerges in every snowflake through the doubling of the original triad of the ice crystal, but is also manifest as often in bone and shell structures,[48] one increasingly recognizes in this way that everything that we call natural forms is only a division of the eternal Becoming according to the eternal laws of form and number, a division that is only through this different from the law that it is never realized without a light admixture of something irrational. For this reason, indeed, it will always remain one of the most essential tasks of natural scientific research to separate the rational in the phenomena of the world from the irrational and so-called accidental, and in this way to represent and demonstrate in all transient things the intransient and eternal laws according to which they had to arise in the way they did, for thereby is repeated in our mind the actual genesis of all these transient phenomena, a genesis the clear perception of which alone can guarantee our mind perfect satisfaction.

But not just the original divisions of the sphere and the circle are great factors for the realization of a number of characteristic forms that can be truly understood only from them but equally

---

47   [Parhelia are atmospheric optical phenomena consisting of bright spots on the sides of the sun caused by the refraction of sunlight by ice crystals in the atmosphere.]

48   See my work, *Von den Ur-Theilen des Knochen- und Schalengerüstes* [1828], Table II.

CHAPTER I

significant are the metamorphoses of a sphere, grounded in the
nature of a sphere, into ellipsoids and double cones. Indeed, there
can hardly be a purer genesis or one provoking more philosophical
amazement in this context than that of the sphere to the ellipsoid
or the ooblast,[49] for, how deeply symbolic must it be termed when
here the original form of all fluids, the spherical drop, remains
indeed everywhere the actual primordial form of every ooblast at
first resting undifferentiated in itself but always, as soon as this
ooblast proceeds to a further development, transforms itself in
such a way that its earlier single centre is now divided into the two
central or focal points of the ellipsoid, thereby metamorphosing at
the same time the pure sphere into an egg form. The sphere and the
egg form are related to one another here just as zero is to a number,
as the original undifferentiated entity is to the first difference, and
merely elementary potential act is to actual act. Only when one
adequately observes this deep significance of the differentiation of
the central point placed in the centre of the primitive sphere in
every egg formation and the emergence of the egg form that is only
explicable in this way does it become clear to us why, already so
early in the history of mankind, profound peoples like the
Egyptians and Greeks valued the egg so highly that they wove it
deep into their myths as well as their artistic symbolism! Proof of
this is the Egyptian saga of the cosmic egg that the mysterious
serpent Kneph or Knuphis (the symbol of divine creative power)[50]
bears in its mouth and that is illuminated when the serpent opens
its eyes or grows dark as soon as its eyes are closed, and similarly
proof is provided by the fact that the Greeks in their temple

---

[49]   [The primordial cell from which the egg-cell (ovum) is formed.]
[50]   [Kneph is sometimes represented as a winged egg.]

structures placed eggs in the capital,[51] in the noblest column form, the Ionian, as a fine sign of the development of the merely technical into an imitation of the organic, a physical embellishment that, through the spirals of the two curling horns attached at the same time to this capital, signified to a higher degree a great mystery that will be fully understood when we, in the study of the doctrine of motions, have deciphered the deep significance of the spiral.

But, moreover, in order to correctly grasp the actual significance of the metamorphosis of the sphere realized in so many bone structures (for example, in the vertebrae, especially those of fish) into a double cone, the deep law discovered by Archimedes must also then be especially borne in mind, according to which a cone, sphere, and cylinder of the same height and same diameter are exactly related as 1, 2, 3. Since from this it results that two cones coinciding in their peaks must be fully equal in volume to a sphere equal to each of these cones in diameter and height, we recognize clearly that the relation of such a sphere to a double cone consisting of two such cones is absolutely the same as that of a unity to a duality, a duality which, however, is itself nothing more than the unity and relates here to the sphere as, for example, 10:5+5.[52] If therefore, earlier, the transformation of the sphere into an oval form started from a mere differentiation of the centre in the case of a possible perfectly unchanging mass, the transformation of the sphere into a double cone (which can now also occasionally develop into a cylinder), on the contrary, is related as an unchanging centre in the case of a mass that is, of course, in itself unchanging but differentiated completely into two oppositely

---

[51]   [Oval and pointed ("egg and dart") shapes adorn the capitals of Ionic columns.]
[52]   All this will have to be discussed in greater detail and partially repeated in the philosophical observation of skeletal structures.

directed cones. In short, both metamorphoses are based accordingly on differentiations, one internally, the other externally, and both therefore symbolize through this differentiation the organic formation, whereas all contraction of the sphere to the five Platonic bodies and their developments suggests ossification (and therewith death) in crystals.

Accordingly, just as up to now the purely regular, rational forms were considered, now the endless number of apparently quite irregular or so-called irrational forms must also be considered in their significance. The latter, however, were deliberately called only "apparently" irregular, for, strictly speaking, in all these apparently often quite accidental and arbitrary structures (one may think of the form of a piece of rock or a clod), it is always the case that, as soon as one goes into details, all their accidental nature disappears, and every factor of their formation was determined only by a, to be sure, mostly incalculable number of influences that are in themselves everywhere regularly determined (as, for example, the influence of gravity, of mutual attraction, of descent and thrust, or chemical decomposition through the atmosphere and water, etc.). Fewer, however, deserve the name of irregular: all the thousands of organic forms that arise through inner vital instincts and can no longer be subjected to strictly mathematical calculation. It is indeed well known that, in itself, the calculation of all crooked lines and surfaces, when they are not indeed circles of spherical surfaces, is bound to great difficulties, that is, that their actual inner law can be represented only with difficulty. If now the elliptical, parabolic, and hyperbolic lines or surfaces too finally vouch for some such expression of an inner law, there is, on the other hand, a large number of others (to which indeed belong all those doubly crooked surfaces that essentially border on the higher organisms) which up to now calculation was not able to pursue on account of their excessive complication, and which we must consider as irrational or incalculable just for this reason, as that through which then—as will now be clear—is proved not a true irregularity of these forms, but only the impossibility of fully demonstrating their inner law through construction.

If we now review more precisely from this standpoint the entirety of all the irrational forms mentioned here, there emerges finally the noteworthy law that, in individual organic bodies, that is, those essentially determined by an inner impelling force, the less that can be known of the above-mentioned purely mathematical and completely rational forms, and the more their entire structure moves in incalculable relations, so much higher will the dignity of these forms gradually stand, whereas the more the rational geometric forms in them are clearly recognizable, this always announces either a lower Idea in general that was destined to be realized here or the fact that through it was evidenced, at the least, a very early developmental stage of the individual itself. The reverse is the case in the case of the general organic or elementary substances, where the law is manifest in this way: that always the attainment of some rational form is presented as the highest of their formation, whereas every lack, or destruction, of such a regular form indicates irreversibly a lower form of the same. Both laws undergo, everywhere that we look around in Nature, the most manifold applications, for when, for example, in the developed human organism, all mathematical forms have disappeared in such a way that nowhere are any longer found even a straight line and much less crystalline forms or pure spheres and the like, whereas just the first microscopic cell of the whole appears in a spherical form, but in the full-grown everything is determined in lines of incalculable forms, that is, in doubly crooked lines, so we encounter in the lower levels of the animal kingdom many other forms that perfectly geometric bodies exhibit, or others (like so many infusoria) that always persist in the spherical form as the form that in the macrocosm remains for the heavenly bodies the general one (although even there not entirely). Nevertheless, in another context, the original form of all fluid elements is in itself already the pure sphere, and the individual chemical element is represented most purely as soon as it attains the really mathematically calculable crystalline form (for example, carbon as diamonds), whereas a metal deposited as a powder or a heap of decayed organic elements must always be considered as a very low form of their existence.

In all the above, it is therewith sufficiently represented that a philosophical observation of the world of forms, even apart from all the elements in which they are realized, presents manifold noteworthy genetic relations and divisions, relations that must necessarily be perceived first if a correct judgment of natural phenomena in general should be pronounced, and I therefore remark at present only that, if deliberately only bodies and surfaces are dealt with here, and the line itself, in its noteworthy differences and significances, is for the moment ignored, this has happened only because, as it had to be remarked earlier already, among the forms the line has reality only as a limitation of a surface, whereas, on the contrary, where one speaks of motion, every direction of a movable body in space realizes the line anew constantly, and therewith many opportunities will be presented there to consider the different sorts of lines more thoroughly.

b. The realization of the form
As soon as a natural element has been realized—that is, has emerged—it necessarily also had to emerge, manifest itself, so to say, in some form, that is, assume a body that can naturally never be thought of as absolutely formless. Nevertheless, the diversity of the phenomena of the physical world is so great that one can differentiate among them those that can be called relatively

formless compared to others. These latter are, first, the fluid—and above all the gaseous and then the watery fluid. However, their formlessness is only an apparent one, since, as was already remarked, on account of the gravity infusing everything that has really become something, every fluid entity that is somehow isolated assumes the spherical form immediately (a mass of air imagined in an absolute void would, as noted above,[53] agglomerate in a spherical form so that in this way all the air of the atmosphere would lie as a hollow sphere around the spherical surface of the earth), and therefore every other form in which anything fluid has been forced must always be considered an artificial form.

The necessity for all elements of emerging in some form must therewith be considered for all bodies as an inevitable necessity and is therefore most appropriately designated by the name of the elementary plastic force of the universe, and this designation will become so much more important for us here in that later we may be in a position to set against it the individual plastic force of the particular and individual organic entities. Thus we call elementary plastic force today that factor of the manifestation of the elements, or that aethereal action of the same, on account of which they are always forced to emerge in some form or, according to the circumstances, under many different forms.

It is this factor, therefore, through which, for example, water either strives, in fluid form, for the spherical form of drops or, evaporated by heat, appears in the form of steam, and that indeed always with the striving to agglomerate in a spherical form, or through which it emerges finally, condensed by lack of heat, in three- and six-sided crystals as ice; further, the same factor allows the purest carbon to crystallize as diamonds, and carbon dioxide to appear sometimes as gas, sometimes, in combination with water, as

---

[53]   See above p. 76.

watery fluids, sometimes (under extreme compression) as a solid body, etc.; in short, every element always has its own plastic force and—despite the transitory nature of all elements in themselves, which, though emergent from the aether according to the Idea of these still, so far as we know, never exhibit a return to the aether, but, existing from millennium to millennium, never disappear or are lost fully—the constant change in the conditions, or the differences, of their plastic forces remains always and everywhere the most essential thing that we have to observe in them.

However, in all these processes, the fact must remain noteworthy to natural philosophical observation that in every element indeed the possibility of individual definite forms is firmly innate, but that it is never determined by, and dependent on, the element as such what form it should take at any particular moment, but that this determination must always be dictated and given by an external relationship (thus the transformation of water into ice depends only on coldness, that into steam only on heat, etc.). Herewith is clearly expressed a very important law whose meaning and significance can be viewed in their entire weight only when we come to an observation of organic life, a law in which the deeper position of the elementary plastic force compared to that of the individual emerges very strikingly, whose characteristic it is to assign every time a special form to the elements that it attracts into its circle. Further, in a philosophical context, it must also be specially highlighted that, just as the number of the special form-elements that could be demonstrated in every body was three (surface, line, point), so also the number of existential forms in which every element can be manifested can never be anything but a triad, on account of its characteristic plastic force, that is—the watery fluid, the elastic fluid, and the solid—whereby then the elements are differentiated significantly only insofar as some obtain more the fluid form for their normal existence, others the gaseous, and still others the solid, and some individual elements also never, or hardly, assume more than two forms. Among the latter are, for example, most metals (iron), which can be present only as solids or fluids (molten).

But, finally, as a repeated sign of the fact that in Nature transitions may nowhere be absent (just as those three formal conditions of the elements also exhibit the manifold transitional stages), it is to be pointed out further that even the elementary plastic force is not lacking in transitions to individual ones. The vegetative crystallization mentioned above[54] of metals, as well as that of ice, are, accordingly, the ones that must definitely be taken into account here, so that out of them, as a result of these processes, once again a very important significance for natural philosophical study emerges.

B. Natural Phenomena in Time

Through the knowledge of the nature of Nature as an eternal Becoming there is expressed at the same time the inclusion of eternal motion in the nature of Nature in general. Since indeed there cannot be, in the nature of an unbroken Becoming, not even a small section in which there did not remain a constant change of every subsequent entity compared to a preceding one (for if both were at any time fully identical, there would be no difference between the two and there would not have taken place any real becoming here), a completely unbroken motion must for this reason be considered inseparable from the concept of Nature, and it has already been said earlier that being and action, existence and motion must be attributed to the original substratum of all natural

---

[54]   See above p. 78.

things, that is, to the aether, as completely inseparably joined characteristics.

But, further, since that which we call "time" in itself is nothing[55] but a constant measurement of becoming by the concept of that which has become something and, consequently, this concept itself is based on the concept of a motion (that of measurement), it is demonstrated that the concept of time always includes that of motion and no natural phenomenon in time can present itself other than in the form of motion.

Finally, if, according to our earlier observations, the first, the original, element is the aether, it will, according to the above, be obligatory to think of this aether, as soon as it is somehow manifest, as being at the same time in constant motion, or, in other words, to recognize the original action of this original element constantly as motion. But, further, since life in general can never be conceived of other than as: rise and decay, action and transformation according to an innate Idea, a thought of God, and since all rise and decay of an aether that has been differentiated, as well as its action and transformation, occurs only according to such an Idea, such a thought of God, it follows therefrom unconditionally and simultaneously that all original motion of such a differentiated aether likewise can never and nowhere be anything but a vital motion.

If therefore, earlier, it was generally declared that "the original action of the aether is life," we can now construe this sentence more precisely and say that all the original action of the aether is a vital motion, or all original motion is generally only possible and conceivable as a vital activity conditioned by a divine will; for a rise out of the aether as well as a decay into aether, and both the action

---

[55]   See above p. 36.

and transformation of the aether, remain definitely unthinkable without any sort of motion.

When therefore, many years ago, Schelling declared very profoundly: "All motion and activity, all vital impulses, even those of Nature, are only an unconscious Thought, or occurs in the form of Thought; but the more regularity is manifest in Nature the more spiritual does its effect appear. The optical phenomena, for example, are thus already entirely a geometry whose lines are drawn by light and a complete theory of Nature (natural philosophy) would be one whereof all of Nature would be resolved into an intelligence," this also very definitely points to the significance of all motion in Nature as a vital motion (that is, of one that is determined by the will of God) but at the same time we are reminded thereby of that much more ancient passage of Plato in which the following is said about the origin of motion:[56]

> That which is constantly in motion is immortal; but that which moves something else and is itself moved by something else and therefore has a bit of motion has also a bit of life. Thus only that which moves itself, because it never loses itself, will also never stop being moved, but this is the source and beginning of motion for everything that is otherwise moved. The beginning, however, is not generated.

But now philosophical observation has further to make clear to itself how diverse motion can be. The most essential difference, in any case, that we encounter here is that between internal and external motion. Naturally, the inner must be considered as more original since the emergence of all particular phenomena was

---

[56] *Phaedrus*, 245 (in the [Friedrich] Schleiermacher edition). Among many important passages of Platonic philosophy I have wondered most at this one since the ancients lacked so many bridges of science to such a knowledge that stand open to us.

possible only through the internal differentiation of the universal aether and since also, furthermore and always, all organic becoming and development is always and solely to be thought of, and arises through, the internal differentiation of something previously more or less undifferentiated so that, strictly speaking, there is really only internal motion insofar as the entire universe must be thought of as an infinite organism in itself. The external motion (as a relatively external one) would then be that through which, among different things that have become, the external, that is, the spatial, relations change and it remains accordingly particular, which is designated by the line and is supposed to be conditioned by that which is called the moving force, although one must never forget thereby that the in itself completely subjective concept of force was applied as much also to the internal motions and has, in both places, occasioned numerous misunderstandings. Further, it has already been clearly explained above[57] that force and matter are really only different expressions for one and the same becoming, since matter cannot be anything but that which in the process of becoming has become something at a particular moment and force cannot be anything but the becoming that is somehow always manifest in something that has become. However, no sort of experience or any reason of pure reason justifies us in establishing a real and absolute difference between these two forms of manifestation and, ignoring that and in spite of the fact that such a philosophical physiologist like Reil[58] declared half a century ago that "Force is only a subjective concept," that falsification increasingly proliferates even now and into the unforeseeable future, nourished by the inclination of recent physicists to crude materialism.

---

[57] See above.

[58] [Johann Christian Reil (1759–1813) was a German physiologist and psychiatrist.]

Accordingly it must be declared here once and for all: "every sort of motion, from the original motion of the vibrations of the aether and of everything that has become out of the aether through attraction and repulsion (gravity and light) which in themselves condition light and gravity, heat and sound, magnetism and electricity, innervation and the motor element up to the original motion of everything that has become an individual entity which we call contraction and expansion and up to the most massive motions that are represented as fall and pressure and thrust—all these are, and cannot be anything but, modifications in the continued becoming of something that has become something, modifications in which we may, for the purpose of facilitating the calculation, temporarily and intellectually separate the concept of modification from that of the modified, that is, from a condition of motion, or force from the phenomenon of motion itself (rather the way I am able to intellectually separate the periphery and centre in a sphere even though both in themselves belong inseparably and eternally to one and the same unity), which however we have to consider always as the single and indivisible manifestation of the eternal Becoming in aether that has temporally become something.[59]

But if above the difference between internal and external motion has been acknowledged as the first one, that between elementary, organic, and artificial motion must be presented as a

---

[59] The deception and, finally, absurdity of such separations raised to reality, such as that of force and motion, emerges very clearly when we find, after further reflection, that, continuing in this manner, we could perhaps equally differentiate between flames and forces of light and heat, between growth and forces of growth, life and life-force, nourishment and nourishing power, etc., without obtaining anything else thereby than a fully fragmented view of Nature in general.

second. Indeed, to the elementary motions belongs every vital impetus of cosmic and telluric Nature as it emerges in the attraction of the stars, the rotations of the planets, in the movements of a falling stone, as well as in those of the expanses of air and water; and to the organic motions all the thousand-fold internal and external motions of individual animate beings, always following the same laws as those above; and, finally, to the artificial all the applications of elementary motion impelled and determined by the whim of individual living beings and of men, such as are manifested in the activity of innumerable machines set up by human ingenuity as a sort of repetition of actual organic movement (one may think of steam engines). But a philosophical observation of Nature has especially to think of these differences in order to fully realise, and make clear in the mind, the original vital element operating at the highest level actually in everything, for all of them are and remain always aethereal actions, that is, manifestations of the aether that is, according to its nature, always in a state of active Becoming, that is conditioned in its differentiation as well as in its motion by divine thought and can in its activity do nothing but manifest ever more the divine Ideas according to eternal laws so that the significance of a true vital motion is necessarily stamped on this activity, since for life in general there is no sharper significance than rise and decay, action and transformation according to an innate divine Idea.

According to this it must also be clear that all internal as well as external motions, whether they occur in the rotations of heavenly bodies or in the circulation of our blood corpuscles or in the rolling of the wheels of a machine, are everywhere vital expressions of eternal divine Ideas, and follow everywhere in unbroken series of eternal unshakeable laws, and the difference between elementary, organic, and artificial motions is everywhere only that they all three represent a scale on which every member is manifest as a potential being of the other. That is, elementary motion is the expression of divine thought in an immediate way, organic motion is determined, apart from the divine thought, at the same time unconsciously by an Idea placed individually by God, and the artificial one is one that, apart from the primordial divine thought and apart from every unconscious individual Idea, is determined by arbitrariness or, at the highest level, by the consciousness of the same individual Idea; but all are always and everywhere only manifestations of the sole eternal Becoming, that of an eternal motion that pervades all of Nature and that is inseparable from its essence, which maintains the life and the organism of the universe as an unbroken chain, but in eternal metamorphoses.[60]

---

[60] If one divides the concept of the condition of motion from motion itself (which is in itself always unphilosophical and, as was shown above, is to be excused only as an aid in comparisons and calculations), and indeed in the form of a force, then naturally all the endless individual forces that we will then be forced to assume must appear as metamorphoses of an original force, and it is noteworthy enough that when this knowledge was expressed less than two decades ago by a young physicist ([Julius Robert von] Meyer, in [Justus Liebigs] Annalen der Chemie), this could be announced—in the deviation of the age from all philosophy—as a "new, important discovery." Recently even Liebig has likewise announced these "metamorphoses of force," but still without relating them to the basic concept of eternal Becoming. When he, for example, says, "the extraterrestrial sun sets the aethereal waves in motion, their force then rests in the product created in the organism; it is not lost; we kindle tallow and wood and release light and heat therefrom, they give out again what they have received, just as the spring of a clock that has been wound conveys our force to a machine. We enjoy in plants the stored force and heat lent by the sun, it becomes operant once again in us; nothing perishes, everything remains, is transformed and in this

CHAPTER I

A third differentiation of motions is finally given through the fact that now those that were earlier classified only generally are now listed according to their special characteristics, whereby we must necessarily return to the subjective concept of force that was already touched on since, indeed, for their specific internal differentiations (thus, for light-, heat-, electric motion, etc.) it was, up to now, accepted to present them not only as special forces but often even as specific matter naturally endowed with forces, and that mainly because one seldom succeeded in providing a full and clear concept of the nature of their characteristic internal aethereal action. But the difficulty of rising to the pure and really philosophical conception of all different, and the most internal, motions of that which has become something lay especially in the fact that everything corporeal was always thought of in an excessively material and solid way and not sufficiently as something that is in itself in a constant becoming. Sound, indeed, can give the best example of this; for, while, in a resonating, sounding body, we normally separate in our mind tone or sound as something independent from the body, we must on the other hand soon convince ourselves that precisely this apparently independent thing is nothing but the complex of all those internal wave actions of the aethereal body-substance itself that was excited there by some striking or contact from outside and now announces itself as an internal motion again also to the external surroundings of the body. If therefore it would be completely unphilosophical and erroneous here to attribute the sum of those motions of a special

---

way the universe appears as a living organism," this is nothing more than a completely commendable explanation of a sentence that natural philosophy was aware of long ago and that it is able to ground more deeply in all its consequences only as an "eternal Becoming."

substance to a sonic matter or to a special force, a sonic force, and if we have to adhere, in the registering of this phenomenon, only to the understanding of its internal essence, that is, of its essential aethereal action, it will soon become clear to us that the same thing must now necessarily be true to the same degree also of light, heat, electricity, etc.

In the observation of all those internal motions, however, we must always include a special consideration insofar as there remains to be differentiated always the subjective way in which we record those aethereal actions through the characteristic organization of our sense-organs from the actual nature of the same in itself. One may think, for example, of light and sound; both are based on aethereal oscillations of the substance and become that which we call light or sound only through the manner in which they are registered by the organism, in the first case by the eye, in the second by the ear; but that which constitutes their real nature consists, on the contrary, really and solely in those very aethereal oscillations; however, as such, this nature does not reach the sense aspect of our organism but is apprehended in such an abstraction only by our mind. Only when we are clear about this difference therefore will it become at the same time clear how much all that really becomes manifest of those motions must be dependent on the temper of our sense-organs—as, for example, entire colours (thus individual special light effects) cannot exist for certain men and how tones are often heard quite differently according to the constitution of the ear and, further, how the flavour of fruits actually do not exist without beings that realise this characteristic through their testing nerves and how, therefore, even the characteristics of light and heat and sound, etc. are always achieved only through the sense perception of the same so that we now sufficiently understand for this reason why a world without men—even in relation to the quite elementary universal life and the rise of aethereal actions in themselves to their physical manifestation—would always remain an imperfect one.

Moreover, every sharper observation of the individual elementary motions in themselves will allow the above to emerge more clearly. As an introduction to these individual cases, the following may be noted:

Since every motion is thinkable only in space, and indeed space itself (as was shown earlier) arises only as the product of an eternal motion and through the measurement of that which has become through becoming, it remains especially important at first—in order to ascertain the concept of motion in all its aspects—to present here the different spatial relations of motion again in detail, just as, in the doctrine of forms, one had at first to deal only with form as such, thus leaving aside everything corporeal.

But everything that is said to move in space must itself, as is self-evident, be a spatial, that is, somehow corporeal, entity. As the actual element of body we had now found (a) its innate limits that can be separated from it only in ideal manner—surface, line, point—(b) its measurements (dimensions), that is, length, breadth, depth, magnitudes that, of course, stand amongst themselves in right-angular relation but, in relation to the whole, are always capable of infinite alterations.[61]

In the case of every such body, one must, in relation to the motion possible to it, always differentiate 1) the motion of the body in itself, 2) the motion of the body with change of place. As regards the first, it is, at the most basic level, (a) contraction and expansion as changes of the relation of the surface to the centre relative to all or individual dimensions, and, at the next basic level, (b) rotation, where of the dimensions one is set as the axis, and the

---

[61] I can, for example, in a cube, consider a line from one corner to the other (a diagonal) as a height, and another line as a breadth, etc.

relation of surface to centre remains the same, but the relation of place of the other diameters to the exterior of that of the body constantly changes, which last motion again can occur in two different directions, that is, either to the right or to the left in relation to the axis of rotation. It is clear that, for the simplest of all bodies, the sphere, this last motion must thereby appear especially as the original motion, because only here, with equality of all diameters, even the rotation constantly allows the relation of all their diameters to the external world to appear most uniformly.[62] As regards the second form of motion of the body, that is, that with change of place, this presupposes always a definite direction of the body moving in the external world, and, in all these forms of motion, there is added at the same time another temporal definition according as the body moves with more or less speed, that is, energy.

As regards the direction of corporeal motion in general, it is always conditioned by the fact that some dimension of that which is moved (thus one of its internal measures) determines its spatial change in relation to other bodies—thus, in the case of a cone, its height determines the direction of motion and it will effect its motion onward in space either with its top or its base, but equally its width or any other dimension can become the direction of motion of the whole, whereas in the case of the sphere, where all dimensions are equal, it must be indifferent to its onward motion as such which dimension determines its direction so that hereby

---

[62] It is easy to understand that one speaks here always of bodies in general in the mathematical sense, where everything that is moved is always thought of as a whole. In so-called reality, a body consisting of tangible parts can, of course, move a part (e.g., a limb) while the remainder is motionless; but every body thought of as a whole in the mathematical sense is constantly moved, and only as a whole.

the onward motion of the sphere remains the simplest, and rotation presents itself as its original motion.

As regards energy, it expresses at the same time the relation of the spatial motion to time and coincides therefore in itself with velocity, whereas, in its manifestation, however, this velocity can be reduced or increased by external resistance. The latter, for example, in the case of that elementary motion that we call gravity, that is, a central attraction, for instance, to the earth, which is not noticeable in a stone that is supported or retained by the earth's surface, but the same stone, without this resistance, would fly with ever-increasing velocity or energy to the centre of the earth and activates this energy constantly by means of the pressure or weight exerted by it.

Direction and energy are therefore always original elements of all motion, for even in contraction and expansion, and in rotation to the right or the left as well as in motion of place, direction comes into question just as much as energy or velocity—for which reason, then, in themselves, direction and energy cannot be expressed visually in any other way than by one of the three essential elements of all bodies, that is, by the line,[63] and thereby it is here that the line (as was already remarked in our observation of form) indeed first obtains a certain reality and may be construed in itself precisely as the forward motion of the least realistic element of all bodies, that is, of the point. According to all this, we may now categorically declare the following: all motion is expressed in the line and, observing the time in which a body is moved through a definite line, there arises for us at the same time, from the concept of

---

[63] The line is, moreover, the essential element of bodies only because the dimensions determining all bodies must themselves be thought of as lines.

velocity, that of energy as that of the other essential element of all motion in general.

According to all this, we understand easily that hereby that which we, in relation to any self-moved thing, call the type or quality of its motion—that is, if it is a drop that falls or a flame that rises, or an electric spark that flashes through, or a muscle that contracts—does not, in these abstract observations of motion, in any way make any change, for all these differences constitute only the concrete or real motions whereas, in the contracting muscle and in the electric spark and in the rising flame or in the falling drop, only two factors are, according to their motion, especially measurable, that is, direction and energy.

Because, accordingly, the line constructed by the forward moving point indeed represents most clearly the element of all motion, there remains now for natural philosophical observation—just as it represented the abstract form in itself in relation to the real world of forms—the task, before it throws light on the most important individual natural motions, of first representing sharply the basic differences of the line in general and only then turning to the lines described in reality through motion.

But the basic differences of the line, in this context, are:

1. The straight line. A constantly self-moving point imagined in absolute space would always describe only the straight, that is, the endless straight, line, for then there would be nothing whereby this motion could be somehow restricted or directed elsewhere. The straight line is, therefore, indeed, as that which represents the most perfect uniformity and indifference of progression, the most original and the first; but, since it never really encounters an absolute void where it

can operate perfectly alone, it exists only as a conditioned line and is totally impossible as an endless line.[64]

2. Directly related to the straight line with a perfect indifference regarding its direction is then that which must be thought of as a progressive motion with a constantly changed or differentiated direction, as which then is necessarily produced an always finite—that is, one that ends in itself—line, that is, a circular line. Just as, therefore, the straight line actually always strives to become infinite in itself, but is not possible as an infinite one, the circular line in itself is always and unconditionally finite. If, therefore, the circle is required as the directional line of a motion of place, this can appear always even there only as finite or, if it should really protract itself further as a circular course, there is possible to it always only the repetition of the same finite line.

3. The first truly possible line, and indeed possible as an infinite line, will therefore be only one that emerges likewise from a progressing one that is continuously differentiated in its direction, but no longer in such a way that this alteration remains always unconditionally equal, but in such a way that this is thought of as continuously altered and differentiated, which then necessarily produces the spiral. Therewith it is easy to understand that, whereas the straight and circular line were completely impossible as truly infinite lines in reality, the

---

[64] This (which so few people perhaps think of) is so true that it remains as absolutely impossible for men to draw a long straight line—since it must at least become crooked following the curvature of the earth—as in miniature it is possible for him (on account of the shortness of the material that is set against it everywhere) to draw a very short line with perfect mathematical accuracy; but the infinite straight line necessarily always remains possible only in thought, for example, thought of as a hypothetical axis of the universe.

infinite spiral, on the contrary, is that which must also be really present—where some occasion is given for its rise—everywhere in Nature, where every movement must, among the infinity of other movements, be continuously differentiated. However, it must be remarked that the spiral line announces its higher, one may indeed say its more organic, significance by the fact that it is no longer single but is immediately divided into many species. It is, according to its nature, infinite (a) in a two-sided way or (b) in a one-sided. As regards the two-sided infinite spiral, it exists as soon as the windings no longer proceed on the same level and at no time contract to a middle point. Such a spiral is the cylindrical spiral and the cycloid. On the contrary, as regards the one-sided infinite spiral, it includes both the spiral proceeding on one level and the spiral that emerges from one such that terminates in a one-sided way in a central point. But even here the different types of motion spirals is not ended, since, in addition, there are 1) that of the spirals winding to the right and those to the left (a difference that is indeed realized in the case of the cylindrical and conical spirals) and 2) that of the spiral essentially bent in a circular form—like that of the cylindrical one with equal diameters of windings—and of the spiral windings bent in an essentially elliptical, parabolic, or hyperbolic way.

4. After the directions of the straight line, the circular line, and the different spirals, there are, finally, all the different finite curves that certain motions are capable of describing, and it is to be pointed out here again that they all never emerge from a single element of motion but are always—like the broken lines of motion (such as light, or a sphere, describes in striking or rebounding)—products of two or more combined elements of motion, which will be so much more

comprehensible since the above has shown that likewise all the other types of lines of motion—with the sole exception of the infinite straight line (that is, to be sure, impossible for other reasons)—could emerge only through the differentiation of a first element of motion that is henceforth unchanged.

So much about the nature of lines of motion in themselves and about motion in general. But how important these general statements will prove to be when we move to the observation of the individual aethereal actions and the motions of the heavenly bodies will emerge soon more clearly in what follows. For the moment, let us turn to other tasks.

1. The Elementary Life of Matter
(Physical Motions or Forces)

a. Light and gravity, heat and sound
That the first two must be considered original strivings or original actions of the aether in its first world-creating differentiation has already been expressed above. Diametrical (thus straight line) contraction and expansion, as the most primordial opposite of motion, is represented most clearly in gravity and light and the rise of the heavenly bodies can therefore be thought of reasonably only in this way that, according to a divine thought in the original element,[65] differentiated central points are set that immediately united as centres of gravity, aethereal masses, through attraction (gravity) in such a way that, on the other hand, the individual masses arisen in this way could not fail to be held apart by a repulsion that necessarily had to be manifested in a prolonged tension of many of these masses amongst themselves (light).

---

[65] See p. 49.

Contraction and expansion, attraction and repulsion, gravity and light, the sun and the planets, therefore unfailingly condition each other mutually and cannot be thought of one without the other. Both are completely straight lines, one appearing only to feeling and the other to the eye. But both are distinguished in their essential nature by the fact that light reveals its eccentric straight line radiation in the finest wave action of the aethereal vibration, gravity its own in an unconditionally centripetal manner, according to the straight line of the earth's radius and of the heavenly bodies one against the other. The completely straight line motion of both, moreover, becomes significant through the fact that the straight line in the condition in which we found it is as primordial as these aethereal actions themselves.

Light and gravity (as continuous becoming) operate on bodies (that which has become) only insofar as the latter are all basically of an aethereal nature; if it were possible to find a body that is not aethereal, it would neither be able to shine nor be heavy. The more strongly a body emergent from the aether is differentiated (metals are, among all that we know, the most differentiated), the more it is subject to gravity (the heavier it becomes) and the more it is opposed to light (the more opaque it becomes and deflects light). The opposite of that then conditions opposite effects, bodies that are little differentiated are less heavy and permit light easier entrance (are so much more transparent).

However, the actual extreme of both characteristics does not appear anywhere, for no body is so perfectly unaethereal (even in the finest thinness) that it remains fully opaque and none so purely aethereal that it does not yet pose some restriction to light (that it would be fully transparent). The best proof of the latter is that even the aether of universal space is not fully transparent, for otherwise—since the heavenly bodies are infinitely multiple—the entire heavens would appear to be only full of stars, that is, be a single shining cover.

For light as well as gravity the centre is really the most determinative—for gravity insofar as all bodies are drawn only in the direction of their central point, for light insofar as everything that is self-luminous radiates in a purely centrifugal direction. But everything transparent deflects the penetrating light on account of the gravitation toward the centre that prevails in every body, on which is then based the doctrine of the bending, deflecting, or breaking of light.[66] Just as, therefore, two bodies standing in a central relation to each other gravitate toward each other most strongly in the straight line from the middle of one to that of the other, the light effect from one to the other will also always be most definite and most lasting along this line.

The new researches undertaken by Moser and Niépce[67] on so-called invisible light[68] offer the most noteworthy proofs of this, since they demonstrate that the bodies that have a special central light-ray placed perpendicularly on their surface are potent even where for us absolute darkness prevails, in such a way that even in darkness a mark found on one surface can be reproduced without immediate contact on the other surface placed parallel to it.[69]

---

[66] The simplest example is provided by the light ray falling in a prism when it, instead of entering straight in, deviates toward the centre of the prism.

[67] *Cosmos: Révue encyclopédique.* [Joseph Niépce (1765–1833) was a French pioneer of photography.]

[68] See my *System der Physiologie*, 2nd ed., vol. II.

[69] In normal light, and without optical concentration of the radiation, an illuminated plate will always produce a photographic effect on a prepared collodion plate set opposite it only as a whole and therefore will not transfer a design drawn on it onto the collodion because here not just the radiation perpendicular to it but the entire radiation

If, therefore, Oken already considered light as a tense aethereal column (first between the sun and the planets), we can now more appropriately call it (especially in its central gravitational direction) an aethereal string and, besides this, consider every such aethereal string (after we have become acquainted with the undulations of the luminous aether) really as swaying and thereby emitting light, as it were, in order therewith to promote also, in this way, the notion always demanded by philosophical observation of the unity of the whole of Nature.

The opposite of light is darkness, though in reality an absolute darkness does not exist anywhere—as already the radiation in darkness presented above demonstrates—since, once the aether was divided or differentiated into light and gravity, absolute darkness is already impossible because, as was said above, there is no fully opaque (that is, negating light fully). Only the chaos (of the fully undifferentiated aether) would be totally dark. Everything that we commonly call darkness is only weakened or obstructed light—shade.

---

operates and appears. In darkness, on the other hand, only the central perpendicular ray (as it were, the reverse gravitation of that point towards the point set opposite it) is effective, whereas all the other rays are eliminated and ineffective in such a way that, as [Nicéphore] Niépce first saw, now every drawing on a plate that was previously illuminated by sunlight is, in darkness, reflected precisely on the prepared collodion plate set opposite the first without the concentration of the camera obscura and herewith demonstrates definitely and clearly the decisive preponderance of this central ray emerging at a right angle over all rays expanding generally and in all directions. One recognizes here the great importance of this discovery, for the opposition of light and gravity is clear to us only after one has learnt to demonstrate such a gravitation in light itself.

The opposite of gravity is lightness[70] and even here the case recurs that such an opposition does not exist in reality as an absolute since an absolutely light thing can again only be an undifferentiated aether, but everything that has become something must also necessarily be somehow heavy since it can never be thought of as absolutely isolated and therefore must gravitate towards some place.

But, just as we now know that absolute lightness and absolute darkness do not exist anywhere, and thus light and gravity operate everywhere, it is impossible for us to think of a time when light and gravity were not yet present, for the chaos is indeed outside all time, and we therefore call the symbol of all possible time eternity, we must also attribute to light the symbol of eternity. And if, therefore, Oken already declared: "Light is the first manifestation of God," this is justified by the fact that the continuing divine creation of the universe from the nothing of the absolute aether can always be thought of only as a differentiation of this aether, that is, as a setting of central points (if it is permitted to divide, in a human way, something that is in itself single into its individual factors) which are also necessarily to be thought of as shining because only through this would contraction, or gravity (that is, the gravitation of one of these aethereal masses affected by this light towards a phenomenon that has become something), become possible, and gravity also here would always appear only as a secondary factor of creation.[71]

---

[70] The relationship of "light" [Licht] and "weightless" [leicht] in our language is very noteworthy and points again to its philosophical significance because light is indeed the opposite of gravity.

[71] Even the recent Bible exegetes have therefore acknowledged, in the mythical creation story of Genesis, the profound words: "And God said, Let there be light: and there was light" as the most essential and

But, accordingly, since light and gravity are from the beginning and everywhere as the true original actions straight line original motions of the aether, they are also—insofar as they remain thereby at the same time original phenomena of all life— the original conditions of every individual life, that of the elements as well as of the individuals. Therefore, just as already the reciprocal actions and the existence of the elements are unthinkable without these two basic factors of the universe, so this occurs also in every individual life of the individuals (and indeed more clearly for our immediate perception), for all becoming of this sort develops from darkness to light and from lighter to more corporeal (heavier), and all dying is a darkening and fading and finally a disappearance and turning into dust and decomposition (that is, an abandonment of gravity, which is an essential factor).[72]

But in this direction the most profound knowledge is produced for natural philosophy from the consideration[73] and observation of the further different actions and consequences characteristic of light and gravity. Important first of all in such a context is the history of colours. So long as science continued with the erroneous presuppositions of light as of a luminous matter or material, one could never attain a satisfying insight into this, whereas once again to a view more in accordance with Nature everything is disclosed in the simplest manner. Indeed, light, like gravity, as they are the original actions of the aether and therewith

those necessarily to be set at the beginning; so [Christian Karl, Baron] Bunsen (*Bibelwerk*, I, p. cxix): "In the beginning God said, Let there be light."

[72] Our language allows us to hear in the word "Leiche" (corpse) too an echo of "leicht" (weightless).

[73] Even in our intellectual operations, we cannot dispense with the relation between light and gravity, thus in the words "erwägen" (to deliberate, to weigh) and "betrachten" (to observe, to view).

the conditions of all becoming, can act totally only on that which has become something; one could say they create the world only in order to appear in it. Nonetheless, now—on account of a necessary internal opposition—on the one hand, again everything that has become something, that is, corporeal, becomes an obstruction to the complete and definite manifestation of light and gravity (for where something has already become something this aether is for the moment already differentiated and therewith not capable of any further differentiation) and, on the other hand, every manifestation or appearance always necessarily requires a certain resistance, an object in which it can appear, so that now likewise light and gravity too can always become or really appear as phenomena only where a corporeal thing, or one that has become something, is present that conditions the operation of both in some way but thereby makes them accessible to our cognition. According to all this, it is easily understandable that light becomes perceptible to us really only through the opposition of the corporeal and, accordingly, where a light-ray passes through an absolute void without encountering any object an effect of light can never be felt.[74] But, at the same time, in just this conflict of light with bodies that stop light and thus produce shadows lies the secret of the rise of colours, that is, of light that is somehow mixed or

---

[74]   Hence the profound passage on light in *Faust* [I]:
        The proud Light that now disputes
        Her original rank and Space with Mother Night
        But does not, try as it might, succeed,
        Since it adheres, trapped, to bodies;
        It streams from bodies, it beautifies bodies,
        Its course is impeded by bodies;
        So I hope that it will not be long
        Before it dies along with bodies.

shaded with shadows.[75] But all coloured light, or all colour (as one is wont to say wrongly, since colour does not exist anywhere as a special thing except for the ignorant, who call cinnabar a red colour), arises in the conflict with a body that somehow alters the oscillations of the tense aethereal string of the light-ray and its shadow, and this indeed in a threefold manner, that is, either as a shining through, or as a deflection, or as a reflection of light. The original phenomena of colour in the Nature surrounding us arise as a result of a shining through dim media, that is, those containing shadows in themselves, that is, through the atmosphere (thus at sunrise or sunset). If the original light of the earth—that of the sun—operates through the dim atmosphere there emerges the positive colour—red, the original colour—and, if the dimness is less or the light itself weaker (as that of the moon), yellow. On the contrary, if the darkness of the undifferentiated aether of universal space operates through the illuminated dimness of the atmosphere, this effects a negative colour, azure blue. In a similar manner, colour is produced by the mixture of light and shade through deflection and reflection—in the first case, through the superposition of an illumined area over a shady and, in the other case, through the modification of the vibrations of the tense aethereal string of the light-ray from the illuminating to the illumined body in its broken half, and this, indeed, by means of the natural dark constitution of the reflecting body itself.[76]

---

[75] It is noteworthy that the greatest poet of modern times had also to be the first who viewed the world of colours with pure, healthy eyes. The many hostilities that he had to experience for this reason are well known. Only recently has he been thoroughly vindicated in this regard in the small book by [Friedrich] Grävell, *Goethe im Recht gegen Newton* [1857]. [Goethe's *Zur Farbenlehre* was published in 1810.]

[76] This is not the place to present a thorough theory of colours, but since this case—on which the multicoloured appearance of pigments

CHAPTER I

Just as colour arises as a product of a characteristic aethereal action and its conflict with our eye, there follow now also very easily—once the significance of light in the universe is correctly grasped—all the other effects of light on the changes of the constitution of the body on which it is manifested. On the fact that light and gravity remain forever the characteristic original actions of the aether is based the fact that they, to a certain degree, condition and encompass all the other actions, such as heat, electricity, magnetism, innervation and, through these, everything, even the substance changes of bodies (chemistry). As regards heat, it exists in such a close connection with light that, in the original phenomenon of earthly Nature, that is, in its tension as a planetary body to the solar, the degree of light precisely conditions the degree of heat, and gravity—which in itself really represents only the

---

is based—is very difficult to understand, the following may serve as an explanation: Crushed glass or snow, both completely transparent as glass plates or ice slabs, appear pure white in normal daylight because they purely reflect, in their microscopic fragments—of which they consist as aggregates—the light that enters without acting on the whole as a mirror. On the other hand, blood—also an aggregate consisting of colourless fluid in itself and millions of likewise almost colourless slivers of blood corpuscles—appears crimson, since indeed the heap of those slivers cancels the transparency here and conditions a mirroring, a reflection of the light falling on it, in which, however, the small portion of haematin that every microscopic sliver contains acts as an opacifying agent that allows this reflected light to appear red to our eyes. Similarly, coal is, as very fine microscopic fragments, almost transparent and opacified only through the oxidized carbon of wood in such a way that the reflected light is mostly absorbed, and now the whole aggregate of such microscopic parts appears black; in this way, the different light colours of individual pigment are conditioned by the change of the surfaces and aggregate conditions of microscopic parts.

concept of corporeality insofar as the same must necessarily relate to some centre, that is, gravitate to it—operates in the case of heat only insofar as the latter rises always to the same degree that the body in which it is manifested is itself to a high degree heavy. (A piece of metal is heated more than a feather by the sun, but both always so much more the more that which is to be heated lies in the direction between the solar and earthly centre.) In this relation of heat to gravity lies at the same time the real explanation of the fact that increased pressure or pressing of bodies (like an artificial gravitation of these bodies towards one another, as it were) produces heat.

Here there is hardly a need to mention that there can as little be a special heat substance[77] as a special light substance or a magnetic substance, etc., but what we call heat in the conflict of a body with our nerves is nothing but a characteristic oscillation of the aether—which remains the original of all bodies itself—bound to the spatial extension of a body. But, furthermore, where this oscillation is essentially different from that of light is that, just as in light and gravity an original cause of all creation and all positing of something that has become something was given, in heat, on the contrary, there prevails a tendency to dissolution that—when heat intensifies to fire—moves precisely into a destruction of that which has become something or, rather (since a true destruction is impossible and only metamorphoses exist), into a positing of some new thing that has become, in which case, as the companion of this new becoming, again light and gravity—the latter, however, in the opposite direction—operate as a flight from the previous central point towards a new one, towards universal space. In this relation,

---

[77]   [Carus is referring to the hypothetical fluid substance, caloric, that was posited by some scientists in the late 18th and early nineteenth centuries as the source of heat.]

and for this philosophical reason, all heating is bound to extension (as the beginning of a disintegration, as it were) and quite unthinkable without it, and again the act of rising as an original phenomenon is—on account of the orientation that is now in the opposite direction, even in terms of heaviness—characteristic only of the fiery, the flame, whereas everywhere otherwise, heaviness is apparent as a falling or descent. Most remarkably, all extension of heated bodies is, as it were, a desire for dissolution, and thereby we understand now fully why the higher the life in individual organisms rises the warmer it is, but also then more quickly disintegrates, dissolves in order, naturally, to reproduce itself anew. Freezing and dying are therefore almost the same thing (since then this mutual play of destruction and formation stops, in which indeed life consists). For the same reason, further, often heat oscillations are transformed into sound waves, for even sound is a sort of disintegration, a liquefaction, as it were, of that which has become something, except that its oscillations have a relation not to light but, on the contrary, more to gravity and do not permit any measurable extension of that which has become something. Heating itself can therefore become audible to a certain degree. (Iron bars heated on one side, when their heat is balanced, begin for this reason to sound.) What we already had to say about light is then completely true, moreover, also of heat, that is, that both become that which they appear to us only through the fact that there is a special feeling for it. Without such a nervous sensitivity, indeed, bodies likewise would suffer the heat oscillations and through this their own extension (whereby we measure their degree of heat), but a heat in the sense in which our nerves make us aware of them as something special would necessarily exist as little in the universe without the living nerves as light without eyes, sound without ears, etc., for which reason I said already earlier that the world is perfected only by man.[78]

If therefore a general natural philosophical observation has made it clear to us how one of the living original phenomena of a differentiated aether (that is, an aether that manifests itself), light, extends its enlivening influence farther and farther and at first draws to itself phenomena of shade, colours, and heat, it is now to be highlighted no less how remarkable the entire wide field of mechanics, with its manifold phenomena of fall, pressure, and thrust, is produced and exists only by the other original phenomenon of the universe, gravity. Of course, one must, in order to see clearly, remove the error that gravity is a special force that is innate in every body and the attraction of the earth with regard to all these bodies is the result likewise of another force, the centripetal force. All our earlier observations have already led us to the fact that gravity and light are simultaneous factors of all manifestation from the aether, and body and weight are therefore to a certain degree one and the same thing, since the emergence of something that has become something would generally never have been possible without the positing of an Idea, about which one may say that it is indeed symbolized in all bodies by its invisible internal centre of gravity. Therefore, just as heavenly bodies arise through a conglomeration of the aether (*sit venia verbo*,[79] since language allows abstract thoughts to be expressed only through images) in the centres of gravity set in the divine thought, so also to every body—be it the smallest mechanically separated fragment— its centre of gravity is its own, and everything gravitates mutually towards one another in such a way that not only planets gravitate

---

[78] Aristotle, too, therefore said very finely: "Nature is bent back by the senses into itself."

[79] [If I may say so.]

towards the sun and planets towards one another, but even a stone
that is thrown, in that it is drawn by gravitation again to the earth
and, for its part, at the same time, draws the earth, although to an
absolutely imperceptible degree, so that consequently in this way,
through infinite concentric radiations, gravity holds the structure
of the world together always—just as light, in its eccentric
radiations, illuminates it always and spans it in its separated state.
The diametrical opposition of these two radiations is moreover
easily recognizable through the fact that, just as light, the farther its
effect extends from the central point of illumination, the more it is
weakened, so also gravity, the closer it is to its goal or centre of
gravity, so much more strongly does it emerge, and this precisely
according to the square of the time of its descent. It is gravity—that
is, the constant ever-striving motion towards the centre of the
earth, even if many times restrained through the resistance of
bodies—which, since it represents the mass of the body in its
weight, moves towards all other movements in a restricting manner
(what was earlier abstrusely given the name of the force of inertia—
vis inertiae), and it is also that which, since it itself becomes a mass
for everything corporeal, also essentially increases the power of
other motions. (A thrust operates so much more powerfully the
heavier the body is that effects the thrust.) In short, in all these,
gravity reveals itself as the true original phenomenon and as (along
with light) the original vital motion of the universe, and this to
such an extent that one may say that every movement of the mass
of a body, however and wherever it may be present, as extension
and contraction, pressure and thrust, projectile and centrifugal
force, will, compared to gravity, always be related only to
something particular (an element or a cosmic or organic individual
being) and accordingly behave, in relation to gravity, always as a
secondary to a primordial and universal phenomenon.

From this relationship, it now follows naturally, therefore, also that all the particular motions or forces last mentioned are always at the same time modified or determined by gravity as the universal. (Thus the movements effected by animals or men are somehow determined everywhere by the gravitation of organisms, and only under this condition does the pressure of water in falling or in flowing at a slanting angle operate, like the wind always partially determined by the rotation of the earth, and so also all motions—or, as one is wont to say, forces—produced by chemical divisions, or formal changes of substances, or by magnets and electricity.) In short, there lies everywhere at the basis of all particular vital motions in the Nature surrounding us, as the original causative condition—as the original vital act of the earth— its striving towards its centre, that whereby it once became manifest and arose.

Further, it must be expressly remarked that among those secondary motions now, as a really internal one, is also that conditioning sound or tone, indeed that it—which especially essentially designates the mass condition of the corporeal world— is related to gravity in a totally similar way as the vital motion of heat is to that of light. (For that reason it has already been remarked above how, and solely for this reason, heat oscillations are sometimes transformed into sound waves.) We cannot think of that internal trembling of bodies whose conflict with our organs of hearing is represented as sound or tone—and which is totally different from every external motion or swaying of the body—as but closely united with the actual nature of the substance.[80] Indeed, all resonance is completely an internal wave action of the mass, where this mass must, for the moment, be thought of as

---

[80] Oken therefore said very accurately: "that which sounds reveals its spirit."

aethereally liquified, a wave action that, like the light waves or the waves of heat expanding the body, would be unthinkable if all mass in general did not emerge from the aether and did not always strive to return to it. Indeed, as this is so, the type of internal wave action and every peculiarity of tone is also measured according to the weight of the mass. A big bell, of the same metal as a smaller one, produces indeed a quite different tone than the latter, and so there will be always and everywhere—like the stronger light of the sun that produces a very different heat from the weak one of the moon or reflected sunlight—an exact relation between the resonance of bodies and their relation to the centre of the earth.

Further, if all the first polarizing of the aether had to be recognised through light and gravity, as a condition of the formation of heavenly bodies, and with it (since the concept of motion is inseparable from all becoming) also of the motion of heavenly bodies, it follows now that, insofar as that polarizing continuously operates not only on the bodies that are becoming but also on those that have become something, even the disposition to sounding (which is nothing but an internal motion) must hereby at the same time be posited in everything that has become something. If we attempt therefore for a moment to imagine the entire original Becoming in such a manner that every external motion of a heavenly body appears immediately to us as an internal one, there arises for us from it also a concept of the "harmony of the spheres" as the original sound of the universe itself, as it were, and every individual sound of a particular body becomes for us then a reflection or a sort of repetition of that universal harmony. Moreover, hereby the cause of that will also be recognized very easily, that once again that internal sound movement always presupposes an excitation by an external spatial motion, an impact or a strike, to awaken, as it were, that dormant disposition and to produce the ringing or resonance. Therewith is clearly manifest in these processes a characteristic motor principle pervading the entire universe, which explains in advance what we will find later, that the realm of the highest senses is divided equally into one sense for light and another for that internal trembling of bodies, sound.

The great opposition of the two original actions or vital stirrings of the aether that we call light and gravity, however, is repeated not merely in the opposition of heat and sound but again, in a new but more distant way, in the opposition of: magnetism and electricity.

b. Magnetism and electricity

The phenomena of this sort of elementary natural life have been endlessly divided and studied by modern science, have led to the invention of noteworthy apparatuses, and found application in daily life of which earlier centuries had no idea. The natural philosophical observations of the same—which has the goal of raising the mind to a total view of the universe—however, grasp only those factors in these motions that must be considered the most significant in this context.

Especially noteworthy, measured in this manner, is magnetism. As already indicated, the significance of gravity is repeated in it just as the significance of light is in electricity; for, where we learn to penetrate more deeply into the great living totality of Nature, we will never fail to perceive everywhere regular continuous divisions of original relations in ever more manifold repetitions.

If, according to this, for the totality of cosmic organisms, gravity is, after light, the really first creative and formative principle, and, if the aethereal action is expressed in the planet most characteristically through the pull of all earthly things towards the invisible centre of the earth, it cannot but be that such an original phenomenon would now be repeated also in manifold secondary and tertiary phenomena. It will then occur that, on the one hand, that structure which may be considered a characteristic part of the planet—as the earthly earth, as it were—also exhibits most definitely that primordial vital stirring of the earth that we call gravitation, and, on the other hand, all earthly elements must somehow share in some way in such a gravitational action. Such a repetition of universal gravitation in particular entities, and indeed the most decisive, is now what we call magnetism, and iron—in which this gravitation emerges automatically in so many ways— presents itself, among the earthly elements appearing as separate elements, as the most basic and truly characteristic element to the same degree that, for the entire mass of the planet (though then in combination with other elements), silicon, as siliceous earth, represents the characteristic element. Besides, because we know, since Coulomb[81] (what is indeed absolutely required philosophically), that all other earthly bodies now operate likewise somehow in a magnetic manner, that is, gravitating in relation to one another and to iron, diamagnetically,[82] and because, for that very reason, the siliceous globe of the entire earthly planet must necessarily be likewise thought of as magnetic, we find in all that most clearly proven the philosophical reason why, whereas the earth in general is to be considered as an original magnet, still iron appears as indeed the most essential material for the individual phenomenon of magnetism.

But the next consequence directly of this insight into this fundamental relation of magnetism to gravitation is the understanding that is now produced quite easily of the necessary

---

[81]   [Charles-Augustin de Coulomb (1736–1806) was a French engineer and physicist who discovered the "Coulomb's Law" of electrostatic force.]

[82]   [Diamagnetism is the cause of repulsive forces in bodies.]

twofold nature of all magnetic operation, as south- and north-polar magnetism, as well as the characteristic opposed nature of these poles also. All primordial gravitation of the earth indeed operates necessarily in every diameter of the planet always in a double way, that is, every extreme of every radius always straining from both sides at the same time towards the common centre.

Therefore, if already in each earthly fragment there is represented, on the one hand, a repetition of the universal gravitation in the attraction towards its own centre (an operation, however, that becomes almost imperceptible since the gravitation of the earth constantly overcomes it, though it can be intensified also to a diamagnetic effect), so, on the other hand, in such a body which (like iron) has the significance of repeating the nature of the earth itself, even the concept of the essential diameter of the earth, that is, of the earth's axis, with its two polar opposed attractions, must definitely emerge. In this necessity, therefore, we glimpse now the true philosophical reason first for the actual polarity of the naturally magnetic iron, or of one that so easily becomes magnetic, but then also, likewise, (as gravitation in a second higher potency) the strong attraction overcoming that of the earth towards indifferent or opposite magnetic iron, as well as the weaker attraction towards merely repelling bodies and its own constant relation to the earth's axis itself, as appears so clearly in the north-south direction of the magnetic needle. Moreover, as regards the special reason of the attraction of the like pole and the repulsion of the unlike pole of magnetic iron, one must highlight here that, since, according to the above, every magnet contains in itself the concept of an earth's diameter with its two poles repeated endless times, that is, once in every conceivable fragment,[83] now also in

---

[83] A rod of magnetic iron is, like all bodies, divisible in infinitely multiple ways; but since the concept of iron as "earth ground" is

every magnet the north and south pole must necessarily be repeated endless times in the polar direction of the entire magnet; but, since this entire magnet is itself nothing but a fragment of an ideal magnet that should itself really represent always an entire earth's diameter, there is innate in it necessarily also the constant striving to unite with all the other fragments through a joining of the opposite poles to a whole, and at the same time to repel the like poles and, on the other hand, draw and adhere to the unlike.

The most remarkable factor of the magnet, however, after all the earlier ones, is, for general philosophical observation, that of a characteristic external motion that emerges many times in this secret internal motion—affecting none of our senses directly— that is indeed conditioned only by higher cosmic and telluric influences but can also, in individual cases, be produced through conflict with electric activity. These phenomena are indeed so noteworthy because a mere observation of free natural life would never and nowhere have given us a direct experience of them and their characteristic periodicity; rather, only sense-constructions of carefully assembled apparatuses have granted us a still imperfect glimpse into these processes. It is possible here only to point back to the original phenomena, though, in the meantime, some very important explanations will already emerge:

As the true original phenomenon, and especially for the remarkable rotations of the magnet needle, we have to consider the

---

innate in it generally and therefore also in every fragment, every such rod or magnet therefore is to be thought of necessarily as an aggregate of infinite magnets, indeed in this way:

N. (n.s.)_(n.s.)_(n.s.)_(n.s.)_ (n.s.)_(n.s.) S.

Therefore, just as in every conceivable individual fragment n constantly adheres to s and s to n, the whole too strives with its S towards the N or with its N towards the S of a foreign body, whereas N and N, as well as S and S, repel each other.

position of the magnetic pole in the great original magnetic siliceous sphere of the earth outside the direction of the actual earth's axis itself, that is, the distance of the magnet, amounting to around twenty latitudes, of each magnetic pole from every earthly pole. Indeed, from this difference it follows necessarily that, if the imaginary earth's axis is to be thought of in itself as constantly at rest, the magnetic axis that cuts the latter at a very sharp angle, as a consequence of the continuous rotation of the planet, moves uninterruptedly in a steady daily swing about the actual axis of the earth in such a way that the magnetic pole of the earth describes daily a circle around the actual pole. But if one asks further what the reason is of this deviation of the magnetic axis from the axis for the daily rotation, we can point only to the elliptic, or the slanting, position of the earth's axis in the earth's orbit, which again can be conditioned only by the fact that the simple gravitation of the earth towards the sun which—if the solar system stood alone and immobile in itself in the universe—would indeed have conditioned a right-angular position of the earth's axis in its whirl around the sun, now—through the simultaneous relation of the earth to the other planets, and especially to the gravitation of the continuously moving sun itself towards other heavenly bodies unknown to us— necessarily had to suffer also a deviation from such a right-angled axial position, and in this way had to produce the slant of the elliptic.

Now, just as it is remarkable, with regard to the elliptic, what enormous consequences for the changes of the seasons, etc., emerge from this simply changed axial position, so also, for the overview of the magnetic phenomena, the just-mentioned daily swing of the magnetic axis and its poles around the earth's axis and its poles is of the greatest significance, since it alone contains the higher reason for the fact that the finer observations of a magnetic needle constructed for such a purpose show how, in the motions of such an axis, changes of the position that are repeated daily continuously not only point to that rotation[84] but also, in the simultaneous relation of the earth's gravitation to the periods of motion of its own heavenly body as well as of many others, produce certain large periods of constantly distancing alterations of the needle in declination and inclination, the complete explanation of which may be expected only in the future.

One of the most extremely significant factors of magnetism for natural philosophical observation, finally, is its relation to electricity, for it is here again that the original relation of light and gravity preceding the relation of these two powers is repeated with exceptional clarity. Indeed, just as the first division of the aether by light had to directly generate the principle of gravity in the cosmic masses forming from this aether, recent physics has discovered that the activation of electric currents[85] in the ambit of a piece of iron produces immediately in the same (but also only for the duration of this current) those individual attractions that we designate by the name of magnetism and has discovered thereby one of the most remarkable phenomena for a philosophical worldview that have been made manifest to the human mind, a phenomenon that apparently is wont to be wondered at less only because its use for goals of ordinary daily life has already been spread so wide.[86]

---

[84] Humboldt, *Kosmos*, 4, p. 122, says: "up to now there has not been found a point (of the earth) in which the needle is not without an hourly movement."

[85] These so-called currents are never to be thought of as a flowing forth, but always as a continuous wave action in which that which causes the wave action remains at the same place. (Again, just as in the case of light.)

[86] A similar phenomenon, that can never sufficiently be wondered at, is that which has already been mentioned earlier and one appearing also

Therewith, it is a true elevation of philosophical observation to become aware here of how that aethereal swing that we call electricity in the copper filament circling the iron establishes the magnetic aethereal action in this iron as directly as the aethereal action of the heavenly bodies becoming heavy had to be established by the action of becoming luminous, for this notion then spares us the entire abstract complex of physical hypotheses of flowing currents of electric materials around every piece of iron[87] with which the unphilosophical theory of certain forces dependent on matter has burdened science in so many respects recently. This significance of magnetism may be surveyed more when that of electrical aethereal action in itself has been explained more clearly.

If we move on now to electricity, we must—in order to conceive its significance rightly—think back to the nature of the aether, the original element of all life, and recall, just as in us, too, the nervous system appears not only as the condition of our feeling and thought in general but at the same time as the bearer of the totally and specifically different senses (such as seeing, smelling,

---

mostly daily to most people—thereby appearing insignificant—the glowing of platinum limestone when hydrogen gas is streamed.

[87] In a recent presentation on electromagnetism by [André-Marie] Ampère, it says: "In order to explain the magnetization of iron by the electric current, we must suppose that electric currents flow around every small piece of iron (?!) even in a non-magnetic condition (!), but that the direction of these streams around the different pieces lying next to one another (!) is a very different one, so that their effects outside are totally eliminated. When an electrically conducting wire is spread out perpendicular on the long axis of an iron rod or is surrounded spirally by it, these electric currents act on those of the iron in a directive manner so that the latter now must flow in the same way and thereby effect magnetic attraction, but fall once again into the old disorder (!) when the former stop again."

hearing, etc.), so also all the different aethereal actions find in the aether, the original element of the universe continuously determined by divine Ideas, their common source. Accordingly, just as every substance shines or is illuminated and is heavy only on account of the aethereal nature innate in it, it is also, likewise, electric only as an aethereal one.

But electricity is similar to light insofar as, for it too, something that has already become something is required for it to become manifest, a body on whose surface alone it develops, either through friction (actual electricity) or through mere contact of two different sorts of bodies (galvanism, contact electricity). The original phenomenon of all electricity for us is, however, forever that which emerges through friction of our atmosphere in the rotation of the earth, between solar light and terrestrial gravity, either in compact masses of atmospheric mist in the form of storms or, in the absence of these, in the form of polar light; but everywhere its nature is based sometimes on an internal division and sometimes on a powerful striving of that which has been divided to reunite with its opposite. Its manifestation is always bound to—just as its original phenomenon was part of—the air, and the form of this manifestation is in itself a heightened light, that is, fire. Every flame is therefore originally an electric phenomenon. The purest and most original electric fire is called lightning or, in a smaller scope, electric sparks, both in themselves nothing but air that becomes the most concentrated bearer of those atmospheric electric aethereal actions through which an electric division (tension) between two bodies is balanced out and is therewith destroyed.[88] If air is absent, or it is present only in an

---

[88] Very wrongly is the electric spark or lightning mostly thought of as something compact in itself that jumps from one electric body to another different one, whereas really the two are nothing but a

extremely rarefied form, no concentrated transition is possible; that is, no sparks arise, but the balancing and self-destruction of the two electricities can occur only through its gradual luminous radiation. (This indeed is the difference of the aurora borealis from a storm.)

The division of electricity into the so-called + electric charge and the – is, on the one hand, similar to that of magnetism and its constant division into north and south polarity; on the other hand, both aethereal actions are different in that electricity (that is, friction electricity) is balanced out and destroyed in a one-time direct or indirect contact with an opposite, whereas the poles of the magnet increase their elementary life precisely through a contact of the opposites; however, both have in common that precisely the unlike is attracted, whereas the like flees, and contact electricity approaches magnetism closer insofar as, instead of destroying its effect through contact with the opposite, it retains it undiminished through this contact.

In all such phenomena the original relationship between electricity and magnetism emerges most clearly, and if we are aware thus that, on the one hand, the electric tension surrounding a piece of iron makes the latter magnetic for the moment (I say "surrounding," not the electricity directly conveyed to the iron, for only in the first case is here fully repeated in an individual case the universal relationship, that is, that of the electricity of the earth's atmosphere to the magnetism produced in the earth's crust) and that, on the other hand, it can be drawn out of strong magnets again through artificial rotations of the electric sparks, we

---

phenomenon hurrying through the air with great speed of fiercely excited and constantly new air masses, just as the ripples caused by a stone thrown into water are not flowing water but merely alternating rises and falls of the same.

recognize here clearly how perfectly those original phenomena, light and gravity, are repeated in these two aethereal actions, and we attain also in such phenomena a clear insight into the deep connection of all aethereal stirrings in general.

And these special instances (whose further complete and individual enumeration we refer to physics) may suffice to consolidate here, from all these noteworthy natural effects, the true philosophical concept as that of a universal elementary expression of life of the aether or (if we may use as a general expression) as that of a common living aethereal oscillation.

But the large vital image of the same as a whole will come to us really vividly only if we, for the moment, first abstract ourselves from all individual-organic creation on earth, indeed even from man and all his artificial experiments with these great natural forces, and take the universe and the earth the way they are manifest in manifold ways in the infinity of cosmic bodies in the enormous motion and life of elementary natural effects. If we venture then to think of the gradual becoming of our planet, how it develops in its constant rotation about itself and the sun, the chemistry of its matter, the reciprocal effects with its atmosphere, and the peculiarity of its stratifications, always circled by electric currents, infused with magnetic tension, illuminated and heated in the different phases and also internally moved by processes that all work towards the further development of its particular organism, we will grasp so much more clearly that only through the fact that we place the above-noticed elementary and universal aethereal actions, according to their nature, in the same series along with the original actions of the life of individual organisms are we in a position to really arrive at a truly satisfactory understanding of the universe, and therewith also at the final goal of all philosophy of Becoming. We must therefore always note and ascertain that "life" can never be anything but "rise and decay, action and transformation according to an innate divine Idea," and that all elementary activity and all effects of those elementary substances developed from the aether remain in themselves infused as much with the divine breath as those in which this divinity called forth, apart from that universal, a particularly individual phenomenon, to which, however, only a transitory manifestation can be granted, whereas for everything universal the endless duration of creation— as Nature and Idea in general—is forever certain in one form or another.

With these words we stand at the transition from the elementary to the individual vital motions and have now to direct our next observations to the latter.

2. Individual or Organic Vital Motions

It can be said definitely that, as soon as a particular and individual life entered the universal elementary life of the planet, even along with the universal (physical) aethereal actions (forces), which indeed pervade and rule the particular as well as the elementary life, new and characteristic aethereal actions had to enter for this particular one that indeed could be closely related to those universal motions but nevertheless always demand an essential difference, although this was nowhere allowed to develop to a considerable degree up to now. Among the most essential of these new and individual aethereal actions is, first, the individual plastic force as the characteristic shaping of an organic mass emerging from the aether and, second, all individual aethereal actions on the shaped organic mass, that is, 1. innervation and 2. the motor principle, in which two electricity and magnetism are again repeated just as gravity and light in the organic plastic force (of the bound aethereal action, as it were).

But we had found already above that, in the elementary world, there existed a law of formation (plasticity) for every special element that remained totally unchangeable for the entire endless duration of every element but always in such a way that the manner in which this law was expressed every time was never determined by the element alone but always by its external relations. But this becomes totally different as soon as it is a special individual divine Idea that manifests itself in certain elements and manifests itself only through these, for—although the existential form of these elements remains under the power and the influence of those external relations—the essential part of their structure and appearance will always depend on, and be determined by, a characteristic internal principle whose effect—insofar as it arranges and shapes these elements—may now exclusively be given the name of an individual plastic force and, to this extent, must also be considered as a characteristic and primordial aethereal action.[89]

---

[89] When one had to recognize a long time ago that there is a real secret power that must work in a conditioning and regulating manner when sometimes, out of a microscopic drop of protein (an original cell), a plant and sometimes a fish gradually emerges, or sometimes a mammal and sometimes a man, or when, in other cases, the drop itself becomes an infusorium, one necessarily sought and found also different names for this power by presenting them sometimes as a formative instinct, sometimes as reproduction, sometimes as vegetative life, etc. The name is here incidental, only it is always indispensable that one recognize this striving and control itself as a characteristic aethereal action and as of an individual Idea, and I may therefore believe that one will agree to acknowledge the name of individual plastic force as appropriate for such an effect. This acknowledgment is so much more important in that on this occasion the question so often posed "whether the organic nature of special forces has so-called vital forces or not?" can be perfectly decided. According to the above, for example, it is immediately clear that that which we called here individual or organic plastic force is a force or aethereal action *sui generis*, which as such is never present in the realm

The first manifestation of this new principle, however, we recognized already in the characteristic of certain substances and elementary combinations[90] for the entire duration of an individual organic world, develop permanently in that very mass and can never and nowhere be originally put together artificially, just as always the same endless duration is assigned to the elements themselves as to the universe so that none of them can be created anew artificially out of another—as little as it can be destroyed, that is, ejected from, the universal circle of elements. On the contrary, the last and highest manifestation of the individual plastic force is when, through the same, the elements ruled by it appear united at the same time into individual combinations (organisms) and, indeed, in such a manner that these combinations henceforth persist as the same temporarily but—following the model of the eternal motion of a constantly transforming universe that constantly partially destroys itself and recreates itself anew— likewise remain in their special circle, for a limited existence, in constant transformation, that is, continuous dissolution and recreation. In this context, therefore, the individual or organic plastic force differs very sharply from the elementary, which, as an eternally unchanging formation, permits the change of different conditions and combinations only as consequences of external influences, whereas the former, as the essential condition of its

of pure elements, where only the elementary plastic force prevails. Likewise, it is easily comprehensible that that, for example, which, as an individual repetition of electricity, we call innervation is not an elementary but an individual aethereal action or force, and so also that which, as a repetition of magnetism, is called the motor element of the organism. In general therefore herewith that question can be definitely decided in this manner: "There are special vital forces that are not present in the rest of elementary Nature."

[90] See above.

internal operation, establishes a sustained chain of self-destruction and self-reproduction by means of which indeed space appears for the first time, in order to make fully manifest the individual Idea borne by it in its evolution and revolution, sometimes truly as individual organic beings but at other times as a chain—again possibly also endless—of similar individuals, through the reproduction of the genus, or as a species.

Accordingly, we absolutely have the right to designate the individual plastic force as the characteristic natural motion, the aethereal action, or force; for, where the elementary plastic force adheres to the element as such and produces only space so that light and heat, electricity, or the elements as such constantly change their condition, there the individual plastic force forms, by means of unforeseeable series of internal microscopic cell divisions[91] of the simplest, constantly spherical dimension, some creation, that is, a whole that is different from everything merely elementary not only in its characteristic substance—which can never be put together in this way artificially and whose equally characteristic beauty of structure can never be attained artificially—but at the same time an internal motion of its existence is sustained on account of which it persists, in spite of constant self-destruction and self-recreation, in a constant becoming, and in all that, besides, attests to a certain

---

[91] Just as light, heat, sound, electricity, and magnetism are manifest only through certain very fine aethereal oscillations, we could represent these microscopic processes of organic plastic force to which all growth is connected likewise as constant and changing oscillations of the substance, as it were, and so, just as the structure of the universe was revealed in musical terms to a Kepler as a harmony of the spheres, we could demonstrate in the cell structure of an organism— progressing everywhere according to remarkable numerical and formal relations—a repetition of certain original relations of the musical realm.

tenacity of existence on account of which it is always able to successfully resist to a certain degree the influences of foreign elementary or aethereal actions.

But such a plastic force produced by the divine Idea of an individual organism or characteristic movement ruling earthly elements will, while it manifests this Idea only in a material form through matter and form, not yet be able to manifest anything by itself at first of the intellectual significance of the Idea expressed in the highest organisms as consciousness. We therefore express this by saying that that formative activity or that formative life is part of the unconscious side of the Idea, and that it consequently always represents in general—in those individual organisms (such as plants) that are not destined in the universe to an intellectual manifestation—only the aethereal action or force that conditions and sustains the manifestation of the organism. For this reason thus it is to be supposed, on the other hand, that where the highest conscious radiations of the individual Idea as feeling, willing, and understanding emerge this individual plastic force will have the further special task, in a Promethean way, as it were, of developing its own organs in which now also the highest aethereal actions, that is, innervation and the motor principle, are manifested—like heightened repetitions of electricity and magnetism, as it were, so that through these finally the spiritual itself may appear in bodies.

All the attempts so often presented to trace back a motor element such as innervation merely to magnetism or electricity will therefore always remain—as one will perceive ever more clearly now—as futile as it will be forever useless to trace back electricity to a mere light effect, or individual plastic force to merely the elementary, that is, the development of the organism to mere crystallization, and to explain them thereby. But this would indeed be the same as if one wished to explain seeing through hearing or feeling through smelling! And so then it will remain the task of natural philosophical observation everywhere to acknowledge those forces or aethereal actions as specifically different and characteristic vital effects of an aethereal being modified in some manner and to understand them as truly united only in their ultimate divine ground.

Moreover, if we succeed in setting the history of the individual organism against that of the universal, that is, the microcosm against the macrocosm, then it will hopefully appear with greater definition that the former cannot be anything but somehow a repetition of the latter and that, therefore, it must find in its substance not only the elements of which the universal consists but also, to the same degree, characteristic universal aethereal actions or forces. Therefore, just as light and gravity, heat and sound, electricity and magnetism pervade and vivify the universal organism and all these cannot be lacking either in plants nor in animals and, least of all, in men, so it must be required with the same certainty that, just as constantly characteristic and newly combined substances arise according to their higher dignity in these individual organisms, now also characteristic, and indeed especially intensified, repetitions of those elementary forces emerge here. In this sense, therefore, one may say that, as regards innervation, its radiation in the organism, like that of electricity, appears as a definite third repetition of the light radiation of the cosmos! And it is then certainly a no less great and elevating thought to think of that aethereal mist out of which a solar system develops according to the individual focal point of the sun and all the peripheral planetary points and their radiations one towards another as the formation of a universe than to think—in the mass of egg yolk of a developing animal creature—of that central point of the highest animal life (the brain) with all its innumerable lines of action of innervation that finally are embodied directly through the individual plastic force as nerve fibres in which henceforth all sensitivity and the manifestation of intellectual life itself are announced. The error of what one may call a merely anatomical physiology lay therefore in considering a nervous system as given and ready and then afterwards thinking of an innervation in addition (as if one were to imagine a solar body first and then attribute light to it afterwards) since, however, just as the Idea of life and also that of its plastic force is always to be presupposed before an organism can arise, no less are the innervation currents as characteristic aethereal actions already conditioned in the Idea of the organism to be presupposed if any nervous system is supposed to be realized. Therefore, if innervation, in this context, were not truly the originally primordial phenomenon for all nervous organization and prefigured deep in the Idea of the animal organism, how would it then be possible that rays of this aethereal action themselves are capable of having an effect beyond the realm of the nervous system—as we are definitely aware of manifold times, and already in the power of the human glance?

But if it has become clear from all of the above that innervation must be considered as characteristic, and indeed as the highest of all aethereal actions, and consequently also of the organic aethereal actions, as one in which the elementary aethereal actions of light and electricity are repeated and for which finally even the reflection of its own Idea in the form of self-consciousness is supposed to become possible, it can already be concluded therefrom that as little will an organic repetition of those elementary aethereal actions be lacking that emerge in the elementary universe as gravity and magnetism. Then it is truly so; and it is the "motor element," or the fibre contraction, that— precisely in the way that a pulling of an electrically charged iron towards a non-magnetic one makes possible telegraph writing for us—explains all the wonders of animal motion by means of momentary shortening of the fibres affected by innervation.

CHAPTER I

But what complicated hypotheses has our atomistic physiology thought of, and how often has it attempted to discover through ever more refined microscopic examination of the muscle fibres that mechanical artifice by means of which the muscle structure is really activated—and yet it was never more successful than one who wished to find out through chemical or microscopic investigation of iron where its magnetism lay hidden! But of course all this occurs differently if a clear philosophical survey of Nature has allowed us to recognize that the motor element—as the characteristic organic aethereal action or force—stands in relation to innervation exactly as, in free elementary Nature, magnetism stands to electricity or gravity to light; for we know then that now, necessarily and solely, one factor must, already through its internal opposition, generate and condition the other, just as positive and negative, light and shade, or, in general, all primordial opposites, always condition and generate one other mutually.

Considered in itself, this motor element, or the organically moved force, has moreover another noteworthy relation to the organic or individual plastic force mentioned earlier. Indeed, just as the significance was attributed to the latter of first extending and enlarging the organism in the form of growth in such a way that its diminution and final death results also in its shrinking and finally its decomposition, so there emerges, on a higher level of its dignity, contraction, in the form of the motor element, to a certain degree also as an opposite to the extension of growth, but is then, however, on the whole, no longer a sign of shrinkage and death but appears now, on the contrary, precisely as a sign of active powerful life, indeed in such a way that henceforth the fibre contraction causes not only a contraction of the organic mass but itself can, and does, cause again the expansion of individual organs as a second factor of higher motion that is itself still produced through fibre contraction.

We are led then to further important considerations when we become aware, in the case of innervation, how this last and highest repetition of light, which itself appeared to us as the first aethereal action generated in the absolute aether by divine thought, now also conditions our own thought so thoroughly, a thought not of course equal to the original divine thought but still a characteristic thought nevertheless that is also to be called divine in its sphere, on which everything that is called human knowledge is based. We perceive then how the thought of that mind whose emergence is bound completely to the innervation matured in the highest product of the individual plastic force, the brain, totally repeats that highest divine original thought that differentiated, and continuously differentiates, the absolute aether eternally through the positing of light and gravity in such a way that now precisely in such a polar opposition between light radiation and thought a cycle is completed in which the beginning and final point, God and the mind raised to God, coincide completely in wonderful beauty.

Having arrived at this high point, natural philosophical observation of the universe may—before it turns to the particulars of natural phenomena—linger appropriately a little and once again summarise how important and satisfactory the results are that its conduct up to now has presented in order to enter so much more confidently, with the light that has been obtained, into the immense circle of individual phenomena.

Indeed, to the same degree that nobody will obtain a living concept of God and his manifestation through the universe in whom the Idea of God did not arise through a healthy intellectual disposition and sustained inner vision (since this could never be demonstrated and vouchsafed to him from outside), it was also one of the most important tasks of the above to develop in the mind of the reader the concept of the aether and of the ramification of the universe conditioned by it, and constantly emerging from it, and no less must it also be pointed to emphatically here how indispensably the actual intellectual activity of the observer must act to vividly imagine and conceive now the nature of such an aether in its full significance, and certainly only if and where this may be really supposed may one expect that the Idea of life can be perceived so purely as we undertook to develop it here—and to pursue it further—in its direct conditioning through the aether (life as the original action of the aether).

In all of this so much, however, may be maintained that one who has succeeded in penetrating into the secret of the aether and the concept joined from eternity with it of life and motion, as well as of the life of the universe flowing from this original source, will also be unshaken in the understanding of the eternal connection between the phenomenon of the universe and the nature of the mind, even if apparently deep chasms may open up between these two and great difficulties of understanding emerge in particular. The conviction that the divine thought that we call a human mind is destined to be reflected and manifested in a similar, but here only limited, way in the aethereal individual plastic force and innervation as God Himself in accordance with his Being is eternally in the being and becoming of aether will lead us—the more we dedicate ourselves to it and the more vividly we retain it in ourselves so much more—to clarity and depth of insight in all aspects, and allow us to fully grasp everything that we generally call either corporeal or spiritual in its higher unity.

It has been the great error of many ages and minds that they, as soon as they had to deal with the motion of the universe, starting from the one-sided concept of a special arbitrarily occasioned motion of individual bodies towards one another, could not perceive and explain that eternal motion of the macrocosm itself other than by presupposing an impact from outside instead of placing themselves in the central point of the task and raising the original life of the cosmos itself, in its constant emergence from the aether determined by the divine Idea, into a constant fundamental vision. Where therefore Plato had progressed so far as to acknowledge that "that which is constantly moved is immortal; but that which moves something else and is itself moved by another and therefore has a portion of motion has also a portion of life,"[92] they continue to help themselves with the supposition of a material and palpable God who gives the first push to the universal machine, as it were, whereby however it had, of course, to be fully impossible for them—with regard to their own mind, which always imposed itself forcefully on them as an immaterial entity and not a palpable—to reach any true agreement or comprehensive vision.

How different, on the other hand, the intellectual vision of the one to whom the universe has become an organism that forms itself anew eternally and to whom it is clear that, in this infinite eternal totality, we have to always differentiate the two originally characteristic factors, that is, Becoming and Being—or the constantly moved aether, the eternal bearer of the incessant living Becoming of the universe, and the divine Mind, the equally eternal Being of the Idea, as that which, according to unchangeable laws and in eternally changing forms, lovingly and continuously bestows on the universe the wisdom and beauty of its own Being—without, however, our being able to venture to think of these two factors of Being and Becoming as being separated fully and truly at any time, or any place, or in any way! If then there enters in this way the image—due to our own imperfection perceptible only very partially and inadequately—of the entire cosmos in its eternal spiritualization through the divine unity momentarily, that is, in

---

92   [*Phaedrus*, see above p. 90n.]

individual elevated moments, really clearly before our soul, we perceive immediately in this vision such a depth of wisdom, beauty and devoted love of the creator for the creation that it must now also soon become undeniable to us how everything that men of every age and sort have sought to conceive as divine worship, prayer and religion and to express somehow in so many mystical and symbolic attempts as something that is however totally ineffable could finally find its true original source only in that vision, and we perceive immediately that a true natural philosophy cannot but be, at the same time, in the true sense of the word, a theosophy.

Chapter II. Of the Specific Manifestations of Natural Phenomena

A. Of the Specific Manifestations in Their Totality (the Universe)

Even if not the deepest, still in all respects the widest, thought that the human mind may think of is that of the universe in its totality.

To declare in what way this thought is best comprehended is one of the first tasks of philosophy. The first question that arises is if it is to be conceived as a finite or infinite thing.

The greatest hindrance to arriving at a pure resolution of this question is here, indeed, our own finite individuality itself, as something that, based totally on finite conditions and acting everywhere only as a finite entity, is capable of really conceiving the idea of infinity only through the highest degree of self-externalisation. Nevertheless, and, as it were, through a characteristic innate contradiction, the human mind is constantly forced to the idea of infinity and rightly considers it as the most essential guarantee of its higher nature that, in spite of its own finiteness, it is capable of thinking of an infinity, indeed of making calculations on the concept of infinity, and consequently may recognize in science itself—as the most positive aspect of its knowledge—and in the absolutely unlimited continuation of numerical series (whether these are thought of in terms of an endlessly growing multiplication or an endlessly continued division) the proof of the fact that the predication of infinity must necessarily be assigned to the universe.

If, however, in spite of everything, there is constantly forced on our everywhere finite imagination the demand of a limitation of the universe, however distant, as a longing, as it were, for some completion of that which has become something, there is posited immediately alongside this another thought, that is, one based in the depths of our spiritual being, of the eternal divine Unity itself, as that which—because in its eternal Being it is a Unity and not a mere One—demands as something indispensable not a mere multiplicity but necessarily always an infinity of Becoming, because every finite number of the Becoming in which that eternal Being should continuously mirror itself would always presuppose a limited nature of this eternal Being and thereby correspond only imperfectly to the thought of the highest divine Unity. If therefore we find ourselves forced to acknowledge that the highest divine Being can, according to its nature, be manifested only in a totally infinite Becoming, that is, in a by-definition infinite universe, we now understand also so much more why even the single divine thought such as is given in the individuality of a human mind betrays clearly—through its innate demand for the conception of infinity and through the mathematical necessity of thinking of numbers as essentially infinite—its origin from a highest and eternal divine Being.

However, in all this it is to be presupposed that the infinity of the universe is never thought of as an external but always as an internal infinity, since only in this way is a possibility provided of truly uniting the idea of a totality with that of an infinity. Indeed, insofar as everything that attains manifestation, thus everything that is for the moment existent, is never to be thought of other than as emerging unceasingly through constant differentiation of that which is absolutely undifferentiated, that is, of the aether, this totality of the universe will now be recognized—on the one hand, dividing and multiplying itself through constant and endless division and, on the other hand, at the same time, becoming increasingly more undifferentiated and diminishing, through regression into aether—as the constant creation of a Mind that is eternal in itself and, at the same time, necessarily an infinite one, since an eternal entity, when it realizes itself, is capable of doing so only as an infinite. For this, once again, the mathematical concept of number is the most perfect symbol and the most appropriate explanation! For number, considered abstractly, is indeed something that is enclosed in itself and therefore finite, whereas in even this concept, on the other hand, an infinity of real numbers is undeniably present.

If therefore we have fully recognized the necessity of thinking of the totality of all special phenomena as an infinity in itself, this leads us now directly further also to the idea of the universe as an infinite sphere, since a multiplicity in which I may assume a central point in every place and of which I know that, in every case, all their diameters are perfectly equal, that is, constantly infinite in themselves, can never be imagined other than as spherical, since, on the one hand, it is everywhere the most characteristic aspect of the perfect sphere, alone among all possible spatial forms, to display a perfect equality of all possible diameters that coincide in the centre and, on the other hand, the image of this sphere immediately rises to an infinite one through the fact that we recognize the central point of the same as being possibly everywhere. If therefore the philosophical observation cannot possibly posit anything other than the form of a sphere for a universe whose central point can be supposed to be everywhere and whose periphery accordingly can be considered only as something that is apprehended ideally, it therewith coincides (as so often in other things) with the childish ideas of primitive peoples and their images interwoven so often into mythological poems of the universal sphere as the symbol of the cosmos and finds therein also the authentication of its great progress in accord with Nature.

One must further also pose the question if the totality of the universe must be thought of as one that is, in terms of its mass, eternally the same in itself or as something that diminishes or continuously increases. The latter because the eternally creating divine power cannot be activated other than through a constant increase of that which is present. But it is now clear in itself that, if we must declare of the universe that it is infinite, thereby, at the same time, the fact of its being eternally equal to itself is necessarily given, for, in something that is in itself already infinite, neither increase nor diminution is thinkable, since therewith a finitude would again be posited.

There follows from this immediately another new confirmation of what was already said in the preceding about the constant increase and diminution or formation out of and regression into the aether, that is, it becomes also clear, first, that this infinity of the universe at the same time presupposes that it in itself continuously changes according to its formations, for every unconditional adherence of forms once created would necessarily eliminate the concept of infinity through the fact that thenceforth now all other than those forms that are present remain excluded. But, secondly, since through this, at the same time, the condition stated above is satisfied that demanded that an eternally creating divine power may show itself in a constant increase of that which is present (though, however, at the same time, that constant change necessarily presupposes a repeated death of that which exists so that in this way the space that is indispensable for new creation may be granted), we will have to consider now, even from this perspective, the totality of an infinite cosmos in its multiplicity—operating eternally and constantly anew in time and space—as being perfectly substantiated.

CHAPTER II

But what remains finally to the philosophy of Becoming to present regarding the nature of the universe would be the concept of it as an organism, that is, as a macrocosm. Further above it was indeed already declared as the character and true nature of every organic whole that "it is the rise and decay, action and transformation of the same according to and as a result of an innate divine Idea in it."

It is obvious here that this conceptual definition cannot and may not be related more, and in greater scope, to any sort of being than to the totality of the universe itself, a totality that is indeed to be thought of only as resting and existing totally in accord with, and as a result of, the divine Being but thereby manifesting itself in infinity through its action and transformation determined everywhere by divine thoughts, that is, in an eternal inner rise and decay of its manifestation, by which then its concept generally as that of an organic whole is proven fully and definitely.

But how much is gained at present for the knowledge of the unity of all natural life if, as a consequence of the above, it must be acknowledged that every individual organic totality is always only a finite repetition of the highest infinite one is immediately clear to every mind—philosophical mind—that itself strives for unity, and, if we can start at present everywhere from this solid basis in the observation of special organisms, we will immediately see ourselves significantly advancing in all respects, whereas that arbitrary separation of the universe into a non-living, or inorganic, and a living, or organic, one can never lead to a satisfying knowledge.

B. Of the Specific Entities in Their Difference (Microcosms)

1. The Individual Organism in General

The consideration of every one of these must always begin with the acknowledgement that it is in itself never a closed whole and is completely unthinkable as fully isolated. Neither a solar system nor a plant nor an animal is thinkable solely in itself but always only in connection with the macrocosm.[93]

No organism as such is therefore an absolutely perfect one, for a truly perfect one must be self-sufficient. But every one of these requires another or more external ones, and most of all the whole, for its existence and can therefore be called relatively perfect only in relation to its own parts or to fragments of other organisms, but we can conceive of it truly only when it is thought of as a part of the whole.

There is another reason no really individual organism is to be called a truly perfect one, and that is that every individual temporal manifestation always remains only a fragment of its own self, because each of these can realise the Idea determining it only in a sequence, that is, within a certain (historical) time, and consequently it can never be said that this or that organism that is manifest is, as it is, itself a whole, just as we have also learnt that in this context it can never be said even of the macrocosm that it can

---

[93] This notion is indeed one of those that have become clear to mankind only in recent times. It lies in the nature of human development to first grasp and adhere to the immediate and to be fully satisfied with it, and hence, in all earlier attempts of science and philosophy, the specialization of view and contentedness with this. Only greater maturity turns towards the universal. The child is an independent being at first; then, to it, its parents and its surroundings are independent beings; only man thinks of mankind.

CHAPTER II

be thought of at any moment in time as fully perfect, since, even in its case, only eternity is sufficient to manifest the entire divine Idea.

Without observing yet the innumerable differences and characteristics of the infinite individual life-cycles that we call living structures or organisms, natural philosophical observation has to raise its glance especially to that which is common to all of them and in what way they, on the one hand, show themselves to be really infinite repetitions of the infinite structure of the universe, that is, of the macrocosm and, on the other hand, are essentially differentiated from the latter, that is, as microcosms.

The first aspect, however, in which every finite organism essentially differentiates itself from the infinite is its rise and decay, both of which can never be predicated of the latter. Every individual living partial system therefore has a beginning and an end, and the factors that characterize these are to be sought for first.

As the first of these is to be recognized the fact that everything that we, within the circle of our experience, call beginning and end, production and death, of an organism is neither a true beginning nor a true end. Not the first, because everything that is present to us as the beginning of an organism, thus even of our own existence, is in itself only the development of something from another organism, something that was at first an integral part of that organism; and not the second, because in the process that we call the end, on the one hand, nothing of this organism really disappears, since the elements are constantly transformed into other living cycles, while the Idea in itself is something eternal, and, on the other hand, in many cases, any part of the disappearing organism always immediately becomes an organism similar to the whole, in such a way that we have first to acknowledge that we do not at all have any knowledge of the true first beginning of a specific organism or of its true end and, indeed, that these, strictly speaking, do not and cannot exist, on account of the infinity of the macrocosm, from which nothing is lost and where everything must only be an endless transformation of something that is in itself eternal.

If, accordingly, we know also that a true beginning and a true end of the individual organism can nowhere and never be demonstrated, there is still the question of according to what laws the apparent rise—the phenomenon—of such an entity, as well as its apparent decay or death and disappearance, occurs.

As regards the apparent beginning, or that which we may, for our own limited existence, call a beginning, we can declare at least so much about it that it always represents itself as the simplest and most undifferentiated, and undifferentiated both in form and in substance. Accordingly, the beginning of a solar system is to be thought of as a spherical aethereal light nebula, and in this way all individual beings accessible to our observation arise as fluid spheres, that is, as ovarian drops, for the sphere is the simplest form and the fluid is the most undifferentiated vital form of a mass.

But just as, in the first rise of organisms, the beginning is always the simplest, so also all continuing emergence, or development, is everywhere necessarily based first on division, the internal differentiation of this entity, and, secondly, on new attraction of similarly simple substances. Therefore an organism can never grow and develop through the insertion of a ready-made mass from outside, but all individual formation will always be only the product from inside outwards in something that is divided into many parts, the philosophical reason of which is just that, generally, all multiplicity, that is, all number, can only be thought of as emerging through the division of zero into $+1$ and -1.

Since from all this it will be fully clear that the essential characteristic of every organic development is only the continued differentiation of a given simple entity, there follows therefrom at the same time that the multiplied repetition of that first differentiation will always yield a significant measure for the level of the development that an organism can ever attain. The more times the division of the individual opposites is repeated within the unity, so much higher rises the significance of the whole, and the fewer times, the lower its significance.

Just as with the beginning, so also with the end! As already mentioned, there is, and cannot be, any true end, any real destruction—or becoming nothing—and therefore it is a matter here, as well as in the earlier case, always only of transformation, of metamorphosis.

Indeed, just as every finite organism is finite in space, it is necessarily finite also in time. The necessity of this finiteness is posited by the multiplicity of the organisms itself. Many cannot at the same time be spatially infinite, for already two would mutually eliminate the concept of infinity, which is appropriate always only to one (the macrocosm), and so even in temporal duration one necessarily limits the other. This process becomes most visible in the movement of a pendulum. A pendulum thought of in an absolute void, that is, free of all friction and all resistance, must, once it is set in motion, swing for eternity, whereas in reality always limits are soon posed to its movement by resistance. So also is it with the internal division of all individual organisms; according to the measure of the higher or lower significance of the Idea innate in them, their development will be either a longer or shorter one, but will always—if they were not already obstructed violently earlier—finally, in the resistance of an external world opposing to them the same strivings from all sides, gradually diminish and finally reach a standstill, whereupon the power of this external world gains the upper hand and the division or the differentiation of the substance is no longer determined by its own inner Idea but by that which is present and still active in the external world, whereby therefore that begins which we call the surrender of its own life, or dying and decay.

Already from the characteristics of organisms considered up to now the essential difference of every one of these from that which is called mechanism, or machine, is sufficiently clear—and also how greatly all those err who expect through a comparison of the former with the latter special information on its characteristic being and life. The complete difference lies naturally in the completely different rise, for, while, in the one case, everything is through differentiation, that is, division, so in the other through assembling (one can express this briefly by saying, "In the organism the whole is always prior to the parts, in everything artificial, merely mechanical, the parts prior to the whole"), in the former everything starting from the inside, in the latter from the outside, in the latter thus everything wearing itself out without reproduction, in the former, on the contrary, everything indeed destroying itself continuously but also always—as long as life lasts—renewing and reestablishing itself; finally, in the former case, motion is innate, in the latter, foreign and indeed a foreign source which we trace back finally to an organism, which is again mostly a man. The artificial clockwork which perhaps imitates many organic movements in a deceptive way to unlearned people shows—if we go to the basis and follow its process in detail—always only a continuation of an operation of a person who put together and directed the special elements of the same in such a way that its own elementary life, for example, its gravity or elasticity, or its electricity, now continues a motion given by the hand of the artificer so long as these elements sustain it; and similarly in the case of the steam engine, mills, etc. In short, we become clearly aware that the real basic principle in a machine and that in an organism are so totally different that no deduction of one from the other can ever yield a real truth.

But insofar as the first sharp definition of the being of an organism represented it as a repetition of the entire universal organism, this already presupposes that the individual parts into which every organism is divided must stand in a similar, though not fully equal,[94] relation to the whole as the specific organism itself to the universal. Now, since we are first of all convinced that, among the totality of all individual organisms, an infinite multiplicity must necessarily prevail, because only through it can the concept of infinity for the macrocosm (such as is indeed always indispensable for it) be fully expressed and realised, we will now also recognize at the same time the reason of the fact that, even for the parts of every individual organism, the greatest possible multiplicity remains always an inevitable demand, and we will understand that the greater this multiplicity appears within an organic unity, so much higher the significance of this organism must rise.

But, just as once again an inner unity is posited within the infinite multiplicity of organic beings so that they all represent— some more, others less and each differently—a repetition of the great universal whole, so also a similar relation between the parts of the subordinate totalities to their relative unity is necessarily present and will be confirmed everywhere in our later observations on these specific life cycles.[95]

But a direct consequence thereof will now be also that, just as the specific organisms are themselves finite and continuously

---

[94]   Because the universal organism is an infinite one whereas every individual one is a finite.

[95]   Only incidentally do I wish to recall the cell as the first rudiment of every animal or plantal organism and the endless repetitions of the cell-form as the basis of every further inner development and division both of the developed animal and of the grown plant.

move towards their death, so also during the life of every organic whole its individual parts constantly disintegrate[96] and and reconstitute themselves and must thereby maintain this whole in a constant inner flux in such a way that it itself develops through this inner movement and perfects its entire life span only through it, a life span that necessarily runs from beginning to end partly in a rising and partly in a descending line and will always represent in its periodicity certain organic relations temporally just as these relations are represented spatially too through a characteristic shaping.

Moreover, as emerges from the above, the fact that every specific organism in its life displays and manifests itself not merely in space but likewise in a shorter or longer time period demands now a sharper conceptual definition of organism itself, for we recognize hereby immediately that not merely the tangible manifestation of an organism, such as it appears to us momentarily at one or another moment, may be assigned this name, but we require another special appellation that can include and designate the entirety of all manifestations of it such as they follow one another during the entire duration of its development, an entirety that is, to be sure, grasped in no way but in the mind, that is, in an ideal manner, and for which the term "ideal organism," as opposed to a sensorily perceived "real" organism, or to organism as such, is the most appropriate.

If therefore we have already above recognized every organism in its individual manifestation as a mere "fragment of itself" and therewith as an imperfect one, it is necessary to add at present that thus only the ideal organism deserves the name of a relatively perfect one, that is, this or that man (including his entire life from birth to death) is always first considered as an ideal organism, his

---

[96]   "The body does not stop dying," said Plato already.

self in fact, and so also then every animal, plant, and heavenly body or system of heavenly bodies.

Indeed, the concept of an ideal organism permits another application that must no less than the one just presented be called significant in a philosophical context. Since not merely the different manifest forms displayed through time of an individual organic whole belong together and are united under the term of ideal organism, but it is to be acknowledged likewise that in many cases portions or conditions of individual organisms, though independent in themselves, are united by an invisible band in such a way that only the combination of all of them must be conceived of as a higher organic whole (thus, for example, all individual men in the concept of mankind or individual abnormal ones in the concept of disease), so we encounter here once again a special form of ideal organisms that is again essentially different from the first, but the knowledge of which likewise remains indispensable for the correct conception of the total concept of an organism.

We may therefore summarise now, once again, the conceptual definition of an organism and the entire schematic classification of this concept in the following words: "An organism is the temporal and spatial form and life of a spiritual prototype or original model and in this respect always a fragmentary and imperfect repetition of the universal whole (the original organism—macrocosm), the significance of which will always necessarily be so much higher the closer its spiritual original Idea approaches the true and highest divine mystery and the more—in its formation and life—its division as an individual approaches the infinity of the universal whole by having a constant unity in all its parts and the greatest multiplicity of all parts among themselves."

As regards the schematic classification of all the differences of this concept, it yields now, following the above, this chart:

ORGANISM

a. Macrocosm

>The universe conceived of at any moment (real macrocosm).

>The universe as a whole in its infinite duration (ideal macrocosm).

b. Microcosm

>Individual organism in itself (real microcosm).

>The totality of all life forms of this individual organism that follow one another in time (ideal individual microcosm).

>The totality of all similar individual organisms (ideal total microcosm of the genus, class, etc.).

So much then may suffice to make clear, in a natural philosophical sense, the concept of an organism and that of its basic different forms. If we now turn our attention to the individual groups of real organisms, the review of this universal will, on the one hand, help us to grasp the same more vividly and, on the other hand, lead us to perceive more clearly and to understand more perfectly its individual forms.

CHAPTER II

The second chapter continues with the following sections:

2. The Cosmic
3. The Telluric
    a. Vital Movements of the Earth's Crust
        i. The Formal Type of These Movements
        ii. The Physical Type of the Life Movement of the

Earth's

            Crust
        iii. Types of Geological History
        iv. First Sign of Individuality in the Earth's Crust in

Crystals
    b. Vital Movements of the Earth's Atmosphere
    c. Vital Movements of the Earth's Waters
    d. Vital Movements of the Earth's Fire
4. The Epitelluric
   First Realm of Epitelluric Organisms
   Proto-Organisms
   Second Realm of the Epitelluric
   Plants
   Original Plants
   Concept of the Spiral
   Metamorphosis of Plants
   The Sorb-Like Plant System
   Production of Plant Seeds
   Relation of Plants to the Surface of the Earth's Globe
   The Ideal Life of Plants
   Decay and Death of Plants
   Third Realm of the Epitelluric
   The Animal Kingdom
   Morphology

Morphology of the Individual Organic Systems of Animal
Bodies

1. The Systems of Organic Plastic Formation
    a. Lung System
    b. Skin System
    c. Vascular System
    d. Reproductive System
       Development of New Individuals
2. Animal Systems
    e. Nervous System
    f. System of Senses
        1. Skin-Sensation as Feeling
        2. Skin-Sensation as Touch
        3. Sense of Taste
        4. Sense of Sex
        5. Sense of Smell
        6. Sense of Vision
        7. Sense of Hearing
    g. Motor System
    h. The Skeleton
        a. Of the Difference of Skeletons
        b. Of the Regular Divisions of the Skeleton
3. The Zoological System.

CHAPTER II

Fourth Realm of the Epitelluric
Mankind

i. Of that which distinguishes mankind from the animal world

The microscopic original cell from which man emerged is the highest possible product of the macrocosmic original cell of the planet earth, but, for that reason, not to be supposed as the most perfect and as one that alone is able to develop the highest individual organism. Already, actual anthropological research can decidedly prove that dispositions to organs and abilities are present in our organization that did not here attain actual representation and activity;[97] a more competent research would therefore be more capable of demonstrating them, indeed of their being infinite.

Now it is remarkable, but at the same time very natural, that dark presentiments in this direction occurred through the history

---

[97] The most striking example of this sort is the representation of wings on human shoulders that has passed into the visual arts since the earliest times, for which I have already demonstrated in detail, in the work referred to many times on the original parts of the shell and bone structure, that the reason for the delight in an animated human shoulder arises only out of the demand that has remained unfulfilled in man of a higher radiation of the original vortex (see above), a demand that is fulfilled so perfectly in the exoskeleton of all winged insects and that alone explains the fact that the wings on the shoulder of an angel appear to our eyes really as a heightening of the human form and beautiful. For such reasons too Greek sculptors were allowed to give to the profile of a divine head a visual angle of more than 90°, which does not occur in a real man, or old Italian painters could diminish the pupil of the eye of their saints and therewith suggest a greater expansion of the spiritual part of the eye (retina) than Nature has, etc.—all perceptions of how perfections of organization can be imagined that were not able to develop anywhere in the human species such as it inhabits the earth at present.

of mankind from the beginning and that there is not to be found a single race that has attained any sort of culture that did not have sagas of higher, that is, supernatural, beings, beings that were thought of always as a sort of intermediate stage between mankind and gods.

Even if we leave it at that, it will still always be the first task of a natural philosophical observation of mankind to demonstrate the characteristics whereby this realm and the individual human formation is so sharply differentiated compared to all other kingdoms, and especially to the animal kingdom, and to highlight its significance.

That, however, in general, of the three higher developed epitelluric realms, that of plants is characterized by the perpendicular direction, animals by the horizontal, and mankind, in the case of its freedom to adopt any position, again essentially by the perpendicular direction, has already been sufficiently highlighted earlier. What follows here from this at first is: only men have generally and truly a stature, an upright position, a *statura*, the *statura procerus*;[98] in one word, he is also thereby the noblest, the *procer*, of the world. Here, however, up to now, a most remarkable fact has remained unobserved—that is that, if this stature—in its total height, as well as in its truly physiological proportions—is measured against both any vertebrate as well as other men, according to the standard measurement (that is, according to the third of the upright length of the backbone), the

---

[98]   [Noble stature. In a letter ascribed to Lentulus, governor of Jerusalem, to the Roman Senate that was translated into Italian from Latin in the fifteenth century, the author describes Jesus as *statura procerus, mediocris et spectabilis* ("of noble stature, medium height and handsome").]

stature of man is really the biggest of all creatures that cohabit with him on earth.

This apparently so paradoxical sentence is confirmed definitively as soon as we establish the comparisons in the correct manner and, if natural philosophy may postulate the sentence *a priori* "that man, in whose innervation the light of the mind emerges, must be proved to be as the peak of all organisation," then the observation is proved here fully in relation to stature too. Thus only men exhibit a normal height of 9½ heads,[99] whereas the erect position of an animal from the ground remains generally rather imperfect, and even the human-like ape in an upright position does not reach more than 8½ heads; thus the erect height of even the absolutely tallest animal on earth, the giraffe, does not even reach 6 heads.[100] Indeed, if we wished finally to apply this measurement even to the numerous cetaceans[101] that never abandon the horizontal position, or to the tall birds (flamingos or ostriches), we would always find bodily heights of only five or six heads.

It is obvious that this noble and significant "stature" of man, as it remains the necessary consequence of his higher organization, must find its last reason in the innervation that is developed here in its purest form; for it cannot be other than that, where a great significance pertains to this innervation itself, both in the nervous system and in the systems that stand in the most precise relation to

---

[99] The "head" is used as a unit of measurement for humans, animals, and birds.

[100] The interesting *aperçu*, that, according to the mass of its own head, no animal that is at all capable of an erect stature can compare with man as being both nobler and also, in this sense, really taller than them all, I myself made in the essay on the comparative symbolism of ape- and human skeletons in the 28th volume of *Acta Leopoldina*; so one may compare the illustrations provided there.

[101] [Marine mammals.]

it—the skeleton, the senses, and the motor principle—
characteristically new and significant factors emerge, whereas, by
contrast, the vegetative systems indeed similarly increase in general
their formative type, but in manifold ways more strongly in
animals than they can be in men.

Moreover, natural philosophy cannot have the task of
demonstrating in detail all the factors of the organization that
belong here since, on the contrary, only a special research that is
everywhere directed by the light of Ideas would be fully appointed
here; but it should in any case pay attention to the most important
facts pertaining to this, and for that reason many details have
already been recorded earlier, such as, for example, the unique
threefold division of the brain structure that is ordered according
to the principle of centricity. Along with a brief survey of what was
discussed earlier, only the following is therefore to be added:

But even if the characteristic secret of human perfection and
human exceptionalism compared to all other epitelluric[102]
creatures, can be given not in an exclusive manner and not in a
single one, but always as a whole and in the harmonious
subordination of the form of all organs under the Idea of a unity,
the skeleton remains always, after the nervous system, an especially
important measure. For in it there emerges for the first time—in
constant relation to the brain—the skull in such a nobly formed
arch as in absolutely no epitelluric being, and indeed as the peak of
the entire form; and in that its inner division into three perfect and
three imperfect intervortices represents, on the one hand, the
numerus perfectus 6, and repeats moreover the number 3 in the
similarly imperfect facial vortices; on the other hand, this division
becomes here at the same time the decisive factor of the entire
spinal column, since 4 × 6 remains, from now on, the standard

---

[102] [Epitelluric = that which is found on the earth.]

number of the entire free backbone, which then finally gives, in combination with the skull and the pelvis, the total number of 6 × 6 vortices of a spinal column completely bent in finely curved curvatures. That, further, all these bones even now, like all the others radiating from this central column, are limited on all sides so precisely by fine, characteristically bent double curvatures in such a way that everyone who had been impressed by just this special character, and just by this, would be placed in a position to differentiate the human bones—up to the smallest finger bone—from all animal bone structures, is indeed one of the most important evidences for how totally different the human type was determined to remain everywhere from all lower types. But that is not enough! There appear, in addition to all this, the remarkable proportions of the human figure, which, while finding its basis only in the nervous skeleton, in its high characteristic regularity once again distinguish men from all beings known to us.

Let us mention here therefore something in a more detailed manner than earlier,

1. that the head, which alone allows fully and in accord with Nature the determination of all measurement of the adult body, is present first through the entire bodily height of the half-mature (five-month-old) embryo and secondly through the entire length of the free backbone in the newborn, or a precise 1/3 of the backbone of the adult itself, and thirdly through the length of the entire spinal column;

2. that this head of the adult is at the same time a precise measure of the hand and foot, and of the shoulder-blade and pelvic position;

3. that the same, doubled or tripled, is entirely decisive for the arm, upper and lower leg, for the height and width of the breast and the trunk; and this will also reveal the strong regular

pattern according to which, in man, each and every division of his organism is determined.

But the concept of man demands further that, in contrast to the division of the skeletal nervous system that is recognized to be so significant, everything that represents the first antithesis of the latter as skeletal skin, with its individual ramifications, be manifested here only in greatest delicacy and (as regards the sensory functions of the skin and the higher senses developing from them) in the finest and most sensitive manner. From this, therefore, and totally in accord with this philosophical precondition, there now follows the disappearance of all shells and scales, all decisive bright skin colourations (of which only the lowest branch of mankind retains the dark blue or brown-black), and the fine characteristic texture of the hair in contrast to the spikes, bristles, feathers, and colourfulness of the animal world.

And in this way there emerges, internally from the high motor organization of the skeletal nervous system as well as externally from the fine sensitive division of the skeletal skin, a perfection of the entire structure that is in no way designated here as a special one just because it is the human, but for whose elevation now philosophical argumentation, with purely genetic logic, can demonstrate the reasons point for point, just as it can be demonstrated similarly that 6 has a higher significance than 2 or that a spiral line has a higher status than a straight.

Finally, then, it is to be mentioned that the human skeletal structure generally finds its final perfection in the fact that even the third division of it, the skeletal visceral system, is distinguished by the fact that the development of the capacity of voice and language most important for the awakening of the mind is possible only by means of a characteristic fine division of the same (that is, in the skeletal system of the windpipe and the larynx, with the cooperation of the tongue and the skeletal system of the tongue, along with the teeth).

In short, if we recall the previously established difference between animal and vegetative systems, we can finally state: "the true man (that is, the human perfection that distinguishes him) is expressed truly only in the animal sphere." But when we have fully evaluated this in its total significance, another thing must become clear to us, namely, that only such a perfection could provide the means to allow the characteristic divine in us, the Idea, to be revealed and to allow the voice of God to resonate (*personare*), as it were, through such an organization raised to the highest extent, and in this way to raise man to a worth that differentiates him totally from all other telluric-organic beings, that is, to the worth of a Person.[103]

If we therefore say here in conclusion: the highest thing that differentiates mankind from animals is that, in the former, the individual is raised to a person, then we have already thereby done full justice to the title of this chapter, and we can immediately proceed to the determination of that which may be called the really human in mankind. Let it, however, be remarked beforehand that a correct conception of that differentiation of animal and vegetative at the same time protects us best from the error of granting the opposition of mind and body too wide an extension; for, for example, if it is doubtless that an excess of material nourishment of the body reduces and limits those sides of the same that relate to the nervous system and, in it, the highest aethereal activity, that is, innervation, it remains nevertheless clear that in

---

[103] This important term is, as is well-known, related to the echo of the divine in man just as the masks (*personae*) of ancient mimes got their name from the sounding through (*personare*) of the voice of the actor.

such a case only two cycles, both organic in the same sense—and
not a merely material-bodily entity and an abstract spiritual one—
complement each other mutually.

ii. The development of the really human in mankind

If the earlier observations have already proved in many ways how
the philosophical saying of the necessary complete development of
all organic entities according to the concept of the triad is so highly
susceptible to manifold applications, now there is manifest in
mankind the highest of these triads, and that in the fact that, from
the original egg and the vegetative sphere emergent from its original
cell, the animal sphere emerges as a second element with the highest
structure, the nervous system, but that then as the third element
finally, in the aethereal action of this nervous system (innervation),
that final and highest radiation of the manifesting Idea appears
that we designate by the term psyche or spiritual organism—
summarized briefly, therefore, we recognize the triad of the
concept of everything human as,

1. vegetative organism,
2. animal organism,
3. spiritual organism

triads to which correspond exactly the three organic aethereal
operations, that of the individual plastic, that of the motor
principle, and that of innervation, or expressed succinctly, the
shaping, moving, and feeling, except that all these—in the higher
significance of mankind compared to animals—unite, illuminate
one another in the spiritual organism that is borne especially from
the moment of innervation and finally attain here the self-
conscious mirroring of that fundamental divine thought, that is,
the concept of a person, which was from the beginning, and can
alone continue to be, the original condition of the manifestation

of the entire organism. Accordingly, it will be another chief task of natural philosophy to demonstrate how the emergence of the spiritual organism becomes possible, just as, first, that precisely will have to be observed whereby natural philosophy alone is capable of becoming the true foundation of all spiritual philosophy.

We employ for the highest of all our knowledge the word Idea, original Image, and involuntarily designate thereby that here the name of something has been derived from a light-like phenomenon, a light-process that can be expressed in itself only by means of a visual symbol. But, just as for every concrete representation of universal and absolute light is demanded partly an equipment that concentrates light rays and partly something in which the concentrating light (the focus) may become manifest (thus, for the former the biconvex lens and for the latter some opaque body), our intellectual image too will become manifest only when, first, the possibility was present in a central nervous system of a concentrating innervation and, secondly, when, from the cooperation of a multiplicity of such heightened innervations, an arrangement arises of giving to specific signs inwardly formed by sense impressions the significance of equivalents (words) in which that spiritual original image can be mirrored, as it were, and be embodied in its different modulations; in one word, when a language has been formed.

Now that in the preceding it has, on the one hand, been sufficiently demonstrated how simply the nervous system in the human organism contains such a centricity from which an innervation concentrating itself to such a degree can emerge, we see, on the other hand, how, in language—as the characteristic voice of mankind—the word emerges and how, in the latter, the equivalent is presented in which every extremely fine concentration of innervation, as well as every sense impression, may be mirrored, and in this way there arises finally from these two causative factors also thought (the inner light, as it were), just as in the realm of external light there arises from the above-mentioned two conditions the image or the focal point. Hereby it is obvious that, in order to understand this fully, one may never separate the two factors but that one has to consider them always as mutually conditioning, since, naturally, without a concentration of innervation the development of language could as little be imagined as being attainable as, without language, any higher concentration of innervation could be.

But, if it is clearly recognized now how completely that thing the study of whose total further development remains the task of true spiritual philosophy, and what we have demonstrated here as, according to its nature, the highest linguistically formed radiation of innervation, are based totally on the entirety of our entire organic being and on the multiplicity of such entireties, it can surely be called the misfortune of all earlier attempts at this philosophy that, in spite of such a great multiplicity of systems, almost all knowledge was always lacking precisely of these most important relations of the psyche, and indeed that that factor to which all things must finally refer back—namely, the relationship of the aethereal action to a temporal aethereal concentration or organization—remained unknown to it for so long, and therewith also the actual concept had to be lacking of all those endless modulations and modifications of the aethereal action that are manifested as psychological life in a nervous system formed by a higher individual plastic force, for which reason then necessarily all thought of thought, or of thinking, especially in its most important relationship, had to remain as indistinct and erroneous as any theory of music always will be that does not have the least concept of tonal modulations, their nature, numerical relations, and relationship to the modulating material.—That is—just as every genuine theory of music will always start from acoustics—so also here, instead of deriving a perfect and clear idea of the nature of innervation and its relation to the nervous structure and then pursuing the aethereal action of innervation in itself—as the physicist that of light in its ever more finely ramified division—and in this way gradually working through to a clearer insight regarding the three basic orientations of the same that are manifest to our consciousness as feeling, knowing, and willing, one tried here always—like Gulliver's scientists of Lagado[104]—to begin the construction of a house from the roof and, starting (to retain the same analogy) from the highest point of the roof ridge—that is, from the self—thus to construct a philosophical system from top downwards to the foundation, whereby one certainly had to fall frequently into the greatest absurdities.

But our thought and even one—and incontestably the most important—organic act of our life, will, especially in its most abstract intellectual regions, will never be able to find a more important and reliable director than that which can be completely apprehended above the genetic, purely regular process of all organic development just through healthy sense-perception, and only this will therefore remain forever the reason why we designate as a "purely natural thought process" always that thought that was not spread just by that mentioned sense-perception but proceeds only on such a genetic path. The purer and more unsoiled therefore—especially in Greek antiquity—all spiritual life and its peak, philosophy, emerged out of a healthy sense-world, the more it tended to raise itself to deep results—even when the preliminary knowledge was very deficient (as also among the Greeks); to reach a pure, measured, and fully clear thought regarding these highest

---

104   [Lagado is a city in Jonathan Swift's satirical novel *Gulliver's Travels* (1726). The scientists of the "Academy of Projectors" in this city devote their time to fantastic and useless projects.]

tasks remained, however, always—where that preliminary knowledge was still lacking—impossible to the same degree that we can now justly consider Aristotle's theories on the world system as untenable and incredible, because all those results were lacking to that deep mind which have been provided to us only at present by sharper observation. Now, if natural philosophy also, further, does not have the mission to study the world of the mind in all its ramifications and to present it fully scientifically, it will still be abundantly clear from the above-mentioned that only on it can be laid the foundation on which a further such study and presentation becomes truly scientifically possible, and therefore sketching this ground plan immediately, at least in its outlines, remains an indispensable task even at present.

But, by proceeding hereby from the law of all organic life that demands that always in the higher the preceding lower stage is repeated again, and indeed through an inner heightening of itself, it follows by itself that that innervation that was determined to appear as the peak of all organic individual aethereal operations that are indeed possible on our planet, namely the human, at the same time must somehow reflect and represent the division of the organic life conditioning its manifestation and itself produced by individual plastic forces.

But how perfectly the reality corresponds to this demand can be easily proved by any deep self-examination. If all the preceding had allowed us to recognize how in our organism, emerging through the initial aethereal action, that is, through the individual plastic forces, according to the divine Idea, no higher division was more important than that into the vegetative and animal spheres, so now also in the entire realm of the psychic life conditioned by the highest aethereal action, that is, by innervation, no opposition will be more radical and more significant to us than that of the unconscious and conscious life of the soul. Then, secondly, just as in every individual organic sphere no opposition is more important than that of inhaling and exhaling life, so, likewise, also for the unconscious and conscious life nothing is more important than that of the feeling and counteracting factor as something that acts and represents itself everywhere then in the most remarkable way. Thirdly and finally, just as it was one of the most important of the laws of all organic development that the latter was effected essentially and everywhere solely through division, we recognize now once again and thoroughly the same in the development of all psychic life as that which can proceed only from increasingly wide division of individual entities, that is, from the division and ordering of ideas.

But if the principles of the division of the psychic life in the sentences presented here in a preliminary way are already most clearly outlined, there remains now to present and sharply ground how, in the psyche, the trinity emerges from the duality. The deepest philosophical basis for that lies here first in the significance of the trinity itself. For three emerges quite in accordance with the above-mentioned law that demands everywhere the repetition of a preceding lower stage in the following higher, whereby one emerges once again in two; and in truth it is only a consequence of this philosophical necessity that generally, in organic structures, three manifests itself so consistently and with important consequences, just as already the natural philosophical observation of the formation of the highest organic structure known to us, that is, of the nervous system, had to point to the significance of the trinity in the division of the brain structure.

If, according to this, the first division of all psychic life could act only in a dichotomic way, that is, according to feeling and reaction, at the higher level the original unity will gradually and necessarily emerge also within this duality, and indeed in the immediate striving of this single Idea toward the divine source of all specific ideas, a striving of the soul that we designate as the consciousness of the Being of the divine, i.e., as Knowledge, and that is further determined to become the highest of all efforts. In this way, therefore, does it occur that, just as we have recognized above that first triad, namely that of the vegetative, animal, and spiritual spheres in man, as well as that of all shaping, moving, and feeling aethereal actions of his organism, now also similarly the triad of all psychic life emerges that acts in feeling, willing, and knowing, and thereby turns to that highest trinity that is the symbol of the godhead itself and can be described by us only as Beauty, Love, and Truth.

The task of philosophy of the mind and all genuine psychology must now be described partly as studying in detail all those chief radiations themselves, partly those subordinated to them, as well as the graded manner of their development; in order, however, that the overview of such an entirety is not lacking here, and indeed at the same time that especially the totally organic nature of its inner division become clear to the reader, I give also a table of the same, containing the gradual development of plants as a basic scheme (see the adjacent table), through the careful observation of which many further illuminating thoughts will certainly come to the judicious reader, of which it must be left to him to pluck the right fruits. The scheme in itself, however, requires a little explanation. The first opposition that conditions all created things, that between the absolute divine (a) and of the especially divine Idea of some—here, of the human—organism (b)—on this is this entire image based. The temporal development and being of some such individual organism is, however, always conditioned by its individual plastic force, that is, the drawing out of the elements according to the inner law, thus through its formative life. The specific idea, however, can naturally become an object to itself only in the aethereal action of this organism, that is, in its innervation, and therefore appears first in it in the form of spiritual organism (Psyche), whose gradual plant-like development this image should represent as much as possible in a schematic manner. At first, sunk completely in the plastic life, the unconscious life of the soul remains the ruling one ($\downarrow$), whereas the conscious ($\uparrow$), on the other hand, moves solely to the primal divine, exactly as the plant always strives on the one hand toward the centre of the earth and on the other to the sunlight. This striving now necessarily happens again starting from the general feeling of being (i.e., the feeling of commonalty): 1. according to the original oppositions of acceptance and counteraction, and 2. according to an intermediate original-striving to the divine itself that is repeated between this duality, in the whole therefore as a trinity, which then remains in itself the reason why we are always able to recognize consciously only the original divine in the trinity of truth, beauty, and love. Each of the three great conscious strivings of the soul, in which the latter first develops into a mind, is therefore directed toward one of these divine rays, and this in the form of the activation of beauty as art, the activation of love as goodness, and that of truth as wisdom; and how then these special capacities emerging in this threefold direction are further ordered in the specific capacity is shown to the observant reader by a glance at this table. But, further, how it can similarly become clear to the observer of the table in what way finally the entire conscious radiations of the psychic life in the unconscious reflect themselves as dream life and in magnetic conditions, whereas, on the other hand, similarly all conscious psychic life is itself always infused with stimuli from the unconscious, seems not to require any further discussion now, so that we do not need to go deeper in explanation of this scheme.

iii. Of the rise and division of mankind

The question regarding the rise of all organic life, and thus also of man, can be replied to by science and philosophy only insofar as rise and metamorphosis are taken to be equivalent in meaning; on the other hand, on account of a lack of any experience, there is necessarily lacking also any concept of absolute rise, and to every such question there are always only mythic responses, such as all great races have always had. If science therefore attempts hypotheses regarding such an original rise,[105] it does nothing but add a new myth to those already present and degrades itself as a science.

Already a few years ago I summarized the results of the entirely philosophically justified research related to the history of the rise of mankind, based on metamorphosis, in a series of sentences;[106] and since, after many tests, I find these confirmed, here follow the first twelve of the same in their appropriate place:

1. Man is the highest product on earth, that which alone was capable of giving to it its significance and worth; the creation of the earth had therefore to precede the formation of mankind.

2. Geological research of the present, although hidden in the abyss of innumerable ages, has unlocked, step by step, knowledge of the earliest history of the formation of the earth and the development of the earth, knowledge that teaches with great clarity the real character of those enormous processes and, far removed from the precondition of any

---

[105] So Oken in Isis, which makes man emerge as a sort of acaleph in the ocean. [An acaleph is a marine invertebrate.]

[106] C. G. Carus, "The question regarding the emergence and division of man," in *Unsre Zeit*, Leipzig: Brockhaus, vol. II, p. 65f.

miracle or violent reversal of eternal natural laws, finds precisely in firm adherence to the same the only possible interpretation of processes which will always be able to be apprehended only with the mind's eye.

3. If we survey now, within the space of a few pages,[107] the totality of the history of the earth stretching for millions of years and ask, "Among such thousandfold phenomena which is the really primordial, the original phenomenon?" there is only one answer: "That of metamorphosis." That means that we recognize how the eternal original substance of the world—if we call it aether, matter, or extension or force— conditioned by the higher and eternal regularity of divine Ideas or divine forms of thought, represents those Ideas themselves in a manifestation that constantly reshapes itself in ever new ways.

4. Wherever and however we follow the history of the earth in its major vital characteristics, we encounter metamorphoses, never a new creation out of nothing; and, just as every individual newly born plant, or every individual newly born man, is as little an absolutely new thing but always only a metamorphosis of that which existed before and itself serving new future metamorphoses, so every heavenly body and every part of the same is an ever new metamorphosis of the aether of infinite precursors of itself, and celebrates only in a new and characteristic way in its present manifestation the eternal wisdom and beauty of the highest divine Mind, and indeed in different forms.

---

[107] A very useful survey of this sort was provided by Göppert in *Jahresbericht der Schlesischen Gesellschaft für vaterländische Cultur*, 1856, p. 222.

5. To one, however, who has been sufficiently filled by this great vision, the progressive emergence, in the history of the earth itself, of the individual earthly substances and earthly stratifications, with all their infinite relations to their waters and atmosphere, as well as to the formation of the thousands of individual creatures on earth, appears also always as the same continuing metamorphosis of the same earth; and precisely in the same way that we consider it a necessary development when from the internally almost formless egg slowly, with all its different organs, the young creature emerges, it is everywhere the same process that allows on the surface of the developing earth (also an original cell of the world, as it were, a world-egg), after certain periods, ordered according to an inner necessity, at first different forms of primordial plants and animals, then the later generations of the same, and, in their midst, finally the highest creation of man.

6. It would be absolutely futile to wish to demonstrate clearly the reason of the emergence of specific creatures on the surface of the planet, and it is here as impossible to make apparent the emergence of the smallest moss or the least infusorium[108] as that of men, since both processes go beyond our experience as much as the phenomenon of light beyond the experience of a person born blind; that, however, all such emergence must nevertheless be observed as a continuous metamorphosis of earthly elements remains a totally indispensable view demanded of every logical natural research.

Remark: In the concept of such an organic metamorphosis is naturally contained, at the same time, the fact that the formation

---

[108]   [An infusorium is a freshwater microorganism.]

of an organic being could never and nowhere occur differently than according to the laws of organic formation in general, as something that demands necessarily that all such development always proceed from the simple to the complex and from the indeterminate to the determinate, i.e., at the same time from the liquid to the half-hard and, finally, to the solid. Never was a living thing created through an assembly from the outside, as the sculptor makes a figure out of stone, but creation can always be only a drawing out from inside; that is, it occurs when the Idea of the creation manifests itself at first in indifferent indeterminate forms and then, through ever finer and more perfect forms, finally brings itself to perfect manifestation. In this way, therefore, it can be negatively determined how every organism, and also the human, could not arise; to say positively how the same once arose will never be granted to a mortal.

7. Just as the law of every organic development brings with it the fact that the farther it proceeds, so much greater the variety of that which is developed, so also the earth had in its earlier life stages necessarily great uniformity of climate and of its organic products, whereas both manifested greater variety in later periods.

Remark: At the time when forests arose to which we owe bituminous coal, there prevailed over the entire sunless earth the same vegetation[109] and the same hot climate; only after the collapse of those original forests and their covering with Rotliegend rocks,[110] roughly nine million years ago, emerged, after sandstone

---

[109] Bituminous coal consists essentially of the same plants in the polar as in the tropical region.

[110] [Rotliegend rocks are rock strata dating back 360–270 million years.]

and shell limestone, new vegetations and a new animal world varied according to the difference in climate.

8. Just as everywhere the organic forms on the surface of the planet have been determined in their character by the special features that this surface showed in different places, so we find at present too (that is, within the short period that we call our historic time) the organic world living in the different places of the earth's surface clearly bears that character that those places determining it according to soil, water, and climate reveal—thus, for example, the polar regions bore and brought forth other living forms than the hot and warm regions, etc.

9. Both in the different periods following one after the other of the development of the earth and in the character of the individual organisms on earth brought through these periods there clearly takes place a certain heightening, or progress, from more violent and rough to more moderate and fine; and just as the later terrestrial periods of diluvium[111] and alluvium[112] can no longer be compared to the enormous and destructive phenomena of greywacke layers, the eruption of granite, and the later emergence of porphyry, so also the first vegetable products of the hot nebulous period were always more massive than the tender foliage of the brown coal deposits, and also the animal world progresses always from the gigantic animals of the water world, and later to the finer flying animals of the avian and insect world.

10. Insofar as, therewith, on the one hand, in the progress of the development of the earth a gradual progress from the massive to higher, more refined, forms emerges incontestably

---

[111] [Dilluvium is a term used for glacial deposits.]
[112] [Alluvium is a term used for recent sediments deposited by rivers.]

and clearly, therewith, at the same time, the manifesting force of the superficies of the planet to new and characteristic organisms also tends gradually towards its end; and just as we become aware now of our own organism and those of all living things that, as soon as the time of its lifespan is further exceeded, the procreative ability of the same at the same time declines and then is extinguished forever, so it may also be maintained that, from the alluvium period on, a new metamorphosing of the earthly elements to special life forms that were not extant before has fully stopped essentially and will not return.

11. But it is now at this juncture of the development of the earth, and apparently still within or before the Diluvial period, that, according to all the results of astute scientific research, the great age of the development of man appears.

12. From the knowledge of the fact that mankind was destined, as the high and final point of all the metamorphoses of the earth's formation, there follows that it had at the same time to find itself in an essential opposition to all other living beings on earth, which opposition then could never be represented other than as that of unity against multiplicity. Mankind had always to be—a realm, a class, an order, and a species in itself—whereas plants and animals must be divided into so many classes and orders and into hardly countable species and types. But though mankind also reveals itself immediately on its appearance as a unity, it is not thinkable otherwise than that it did not appear as a one, that is, as one man, but, analogous to the most specific character of Nature, which is activated everywhere in endless life-cells, mankind also emerged, as soon as its moment of manifestation had arrived, likewise in a multiplicity, and thus, further, according to the universal natural laws, in different places on the earth

and, subject to different influences of climate everywhere, once again in different forms (primordial races).

If we now proceed further from the twelfth major result that has been summarized here aphoristically, a healthy natural philosophy, in relation to the internal difference of the primordial races of man that has now to be explained, cannot but presuppose that mankind, insofar as it emerged doubtlessly as the highest and final product of the earth on the superficies of the planet, could receive its true internal division only from the different conditions of this planet itself. But if there can be no doubt that for the entire earth, according to its planetary nature, there is no more important and more determinative relationship than that to the sun, as that from which it emerges and is maintained ceaselessly in the manifold conditions of illumination of day and night, eastern and western twilight, that constantly change one into the other, so it is obvious that there is also no difference that is more important for the division of human primordial races than that according to races of the day, of the night, and of the eastern and western twilight in a mankind[113] that is always changing in its individuals, that is,

---

[113]   Around twenty years ago this notion was first decided expressly by me in the first edition of my *System der Physiologie*, and all my later researches, i.e., on the *Symbolik der menschlichen Gestalt* [1853], could only present and confirm it further. I then—after a prolific author and literary pirate attempted to present it as his own in one of his own works—dealt with it particularly in my *Festschrift zu Goethe's hundertjährigem Geburtstage*, 1849, "über die verschiedene geistige Befähigung der einzelnen Stämme der Menschheit," where it received special acknowledgement from, among others, also [Franz Georg von] Lassaulx (see his *Versuch einer Philosophie der Geschichte*). Most of my later works then introduce elaborately a new principle of division and, indeed, the more a philosophical view of anthropology

newly emerging and disappearing—a division that is clearly realized then in the especially intelligent Caucasian-European, light-coloured races; further, in the lowest, intellectually dull and black-coloured African races; and, yet further, in the more phlegmatic-materialistic, yellow-coloured Asiatic races; and finally in the coarsely active, more or less copper-coloured American races.

But it is another philosophically demanded necessity that, if we recognize it generally as a law of all organic sequence that the higher formation somehow repeats and represents the preceding lower in itself, mankind also, in that it incontestably represents the highest of all epitelluric formations, retain in its inner differences clear memories of the differences of that which has preceded it on earth. But this law is clearly fulfilled at first by the fact that mankind, which as a unity stands against the immeasurable multiplicity of species of all other epitelluric living beings, also represents this immeasurability most decidedly through a quite unlimited multiplicity of individuals that continuously increases in every generation, individuals that for this reason evidence this multiplicity in no way merely through another product of its formative life every time but, as soon as it has attained some mature life condition, chiefly through a difference of spiritual development. The higher and scientific reason why, from the beginning, there has prevailed, and must prevail, a totally immeasurable multiplicity of forms and characters in the human species is accordingly proved here once and for all, and everything thereby points back always to the fact that mankind—which in itself, as a multiplicity, conditions only the possibility of the higher

---

gains ground the more generally must one recognize this division as the most essential.

spiritual development of individuals[114]—can also be imagined as a whole that is opposed to animality.

Further, the divisions of all epitelluric life will also likewise be recognizable once again in definite broad divisions within the internal divisions of mankind. First, as regards the major races, it is not difficult to demonstrate that even the fourfold division of the same that has been explained above, produced by the four different illumination conditions of the planet, at the same time remarkably points back to the four kingdoms of all epitelluric phenomena, so that the races of the night, through their indifferent undeveloped nature and their dull intellects, recall the proto-organisms, whereas the on-the-whole quite weaker and more phlegmatic eastern twilight races remain analogues of plants, and the harsher and active western twilight races, on the other hand, stand more in the company of the animal kingdom, and only the daylight races particularly represent in themselves mankind.

But that is not all! In that mankind is really born anew in every individual, that fourfold division is itself reflected again in the four developmental stages of each individual; indeed, it is divided quite patently into the two opposed conditions of day and night, in that the embryo period spent entirely in the night of the uterine life determines the first condition just as the period of the fully mature man realizes the second condition, whereas the period of childhood recalls the eastern twilight races in the same way that that of the decrepitude of old age the western twilight races of America, increasingly more susceptible to extinction. But finally also all life of the individual man is divided naturally into a diurnal and nocturnal side, in that, in the changing conditions of sleep and

---

[114] Every individual, even the best organized, will reach the height of his psychic capacities only under the condition of the cooperation of other individuals.

wakefulness, the generally unconscious period of embryonic life and the conscious period of the adult man are always repeated and represented. Indeed, so great is the deep consequence of Nature that often invites the happy amazement of the philosophical researcher that once again precisely these same four developmental stages of human individuality that have been designated earlier as embryonic, youthful, mature, and senile must also become significant for the division of spiritual individuality in all mature mankind in general. Indeed, it does not require a very broad and sharp knowledge of men to recognize clearly how in those unfortunate people whom we call idiots is expressed only an embryonic human condition, just as, further, we meet not seldom in life men who, through their undeveloped, limited character, through all the stages of their life, recall equally as clearly the elementary condition of childhood, as we are conscious in others— and already in their youth—of the incompetence, timidity, pedantry, and the entire impoverished life of a dead old man, whereas, on the whole, those always remain a minority who can be accepted as genuine representatives of the truly adult period of life, a gradation that is finally repeated in the four stages of intellectual energy that I have already designated in my *Symbolik der menschlichen Gestalt* as those of the idiot, of elementary mankind, of talent, and finally of genius.

But now, just as all the divisions presented up to now decidedly characterize, at the same time, mankind in its position compared to animals, so also its most universal and deep division, that is, that according to sex, presents likewise many important factors for the characteristic exceptional position of man. The first of these is represented in the discreet equal number of individuals of both sexes which, in spite of fluctuations in individual cases, is on the whole maintained with such a perfect constancy since, while in families very often a decisive preponderance of one or the other sex appears, still always, when large numbers of contemporaneous births or those following one another immediately through long periods of time are reckoned, the proportion of twenty female to a little over twenty-one male births presents itself definitely once again.

Remark: Precisely the fact that this law first discovered by Hufeland[115] is never expressed with mathematical sharpness but always through fractions—which gradually equal one another once again when the mortality of the first and following life years among boys tend to be longer than among girls—remains here of the greatest significance and raises this case to one of the most suitable to correctly evaluate the relationship of other natural laws to natural phenomena.

Moreover, just as it is everywhere a philosophical necessity that a natural law is susceptible to manifold applications, the relationships of this numerical law also operate even further; for, if, on the one hand, the only moral significance of monogamy—with all its important consequences for a mutual promotion of the development of the psyche—follows directly therefrom, at the same time a retrospective view of the very manifold relations of the proportions of the sexes among animals leads to many other important sorts of knowledge. If, for example, it is to be supposed that, with the rise in organization, the differences that were earlier often uncountable between the number of individuals of one sex and the other will stop, in order then to allow, in the highest species, a prevalence of equal numbers of the sexes and a return to monogamy as a normal relationship, it will further be established, with noteworthy connection to the above law, that then generally

---

[115] [Christoph Hufeland (1762–1836) was a German physician who was interested in human longevity. His writings include *Makrobiotik oder Die Kunst, das menschliche Leben zu verlängern* (1796).]

the immoderate proliferation has to stop and, on the contrary, the existing situation of procreation through simple births has to appear.

It is however a necessary consequence that such an important division as this in the realm of the sexes can now never fail to introduce other further divisions of the great totality of mankind of which the most significant will be that through it indeed— through the appearance of the new opposites of parents and children, grandparents and grandchildren—an essential prototype is henceforth given for that organization which then must contain further the still closer conditions of every higher human communal life that develops—that is, to the state. But, insofar as for both the family and for the state a continuous division conditioned by sexual procreation appears necessarily as the first condition, we are thereby reminded once again of that law earlier presented and explained that in general no manifestation of any organic being is to be thought of other than as through division, and so we find here too how every healthy and clear philosophical observation always develops into a whole that is everywhere intertwined and in this way returns to its beginning.

But it must be finally highlighted how the great opposition that governs all human life between male and female individuality does not fail even now to be remarkably reflected—partly, in certain opposites of individual characters, so that now even in the members of one and the same sex one must again distinguish if one or the other nature predominates (there are therefore so many manly natures among women as womanly or effeminate among men) and, partly, that difference itself can also be used as proof of certain general contrasts in mankind, for which reason then also the either more active or passive character of entire races in a certain situation, under the necessary restrictions, remains suited likewise to allow a discernment of two such subdivisions within mankind.

Only when therewith a clear philosophical overview of the realm of all mankind in all its phases has been attained will one adopt the correct viewpoint in order to sketch, starting from it, the entire appropriate outline of that ideal whole which alone is suited to allow individual men to reach the height of spiritual development that was originally destined for them, that is, that of the state, a subject that for that very reason is to be taken up and studied now as the final and most significant task of all philosophy of becoming.

iv. On the organism of the state

The state, observed as an organic whole, is one of the ideal organisms and is, in this context, to be compared to the individual living man only insofar as we conceive the latter too as an ideal whole, that is, as that unit which, in its constant new formation and death of all individual bodily atoms from the beginning of childhood to old age, manifests itself in an unceasing metamorphosis. If, accordingly, the individual man, taken as a unit of its own entire history, is to be considered always as the first prototype of the state, the family—also according to the entirety of its life—remains the second, and only when finally from the family itself, through continuous rise and fall of individual members, gradually a people arises do we see how here also a third development of such an ideal unit presents the essential and characteristic condition for the state to emerge in and from the same, that is, from the people itself.

But, just as we find that the individual man always becomes a real man only through the fact that from his inner life and, at the same time, through his life in a greater whole, the really human, that is, the self-conscious mind, develops, so also a people becomes a state only through the fact that in its entirety there arises a self-consciousness, that is, that that divine Idea that had been embodied in mankind in general and in one human grouping in particular now attains here also its own enduring consciousness but herewith repeats, in the highest sense, that which had prepared itself in more material phenomena in the lowest stages of epitelluric creatures, first through a really organic conjointness (phylloclade trees and zoophytes) and then through a merely ideal unification of many (bee swarms and herds).

Remark: In the same way that anthropology presents manifold examples of individual men in whom the self-consciousness, for some reason or the other, is never fully realized, so that such individuals, in their anomalous manifestation, stand mostly lower than animals, a race in which a higher consciousness and therewith the Idea of the state had never been developed, or only in a rudimentary manner, is always an anomalous and sad entirety, as has been sufficiently manifested, in manifold and frightening ways, where all life conditions point to a lower stage— among the peoples of the night, for example.

Just as, consequently, the developmental process from the unconscious to the conscious, and indeed as to the three essential forms of the latter as consciousness of the world, self-consciousness, and consciousness of God, remains entirely characteristic and the highest life-mission of every individual man, it remains also necessary for the state. And only a political life that has really infused and inspired its people in all these three directions then, and indeed only through this, elevates a great people not only to the concept of a state but, at the same time, to that of a nation.

Remark: From what has been said above one understands easily why the concept and spirit of a nation cannot emerge also out of a small race. On the one hand it is to be highlighted here that the greater the multiplicity is that is contained in this concept the more the dignity of the individual generally and necessarily rises; on the other hand, one may find recalled here once again the first prototype of the state, that is, the individual man, as that in which that significant spiritual development of its essential aethereal action—of innervation—is only conditioned by that higher individual plastic force that made possible a finer nervous system and larger brain; for, just as, without a larger, more significant brain structure displaying innumerable nerve cells, an intellectual life would generally have been impossible, so the strength and decisiveness of a national self-consciousness and therewith, at the same time, the concept of a perfect state are founded only through many millions of individual minds that truly unite in the focal point of an Idea.

But wherein is the self-consciousness of political life expressed most purely and unmistakably?—certainly only in the fact that that divine Idea or prototype of a truly human communal life lying deep in the nature of mankind and of the state becomes manifest in the mind of individuals, highly capable individuals, and now gradually emerges with ever increasing clarity in the form of Law, and indeed only a national life ordered through laws will be that through which the concept of a people is raised to that of a state.

Precisely in the same way that we find that the concept of the real organism is generally realized in the fact that a certain divine Idea operates and manifests itself in the birth and death, action and transformation of the same in such a way that, on account of learning, we are able to establish the inner Idea even as the external law of such an organism, so too the realization of an ideal organism like that of the state is similarly possible only through the fact that the inner Idea of the same becomes manifest in the form of external laws and that therefrom its further development through strict supervision and implementation of these laws is everywhere activated and quickened.

The state in this context has, with regard to its rise, a great similarity to the ideal organism of language and for that reason attains its realization generally only under the condition of a language that developed earlier or at the same time; for, just as the most personal individuality of a people—as it were, the special natural voice of precisely this human race—slowly develops first from the unconscious and involuntary cooperation of many individuals and then, through the influence of especially illuminated minds, develops more richly according to its material content and more perfectly according to its regulations, so there arises in a people, also at first unconsciously and involuntarily, the arrangement to a certain order, even if at first still crude and insufficient, until, in especially illuminated individuals, that is, in those who have attained a higher self- and God-consciousness, the knowledge of the innermost Idea precisely of this national life rises ever more clearly and indeed in such a way that it may be given words and expressed, and established, as law, wherewith immediately and simultaneously the beginning of a political life appears.

Remark: Only in this way can be explained the fact, present in all peoples developing originally to a real political life, of an almost divine honouring of its great legislators (a Moses, Lycurgus,[116] Solon,[117] Confucius); for every people cultivated to a higher worth recognized, sometime dimly, at other times clearly, how much it owed to these minds in this context and that, without such a cultivation, it could not have raised itself out of the night of popular unconsciousness to the daylight of true political life.

But, in directing our attention more sharply to the process of metamorphosis of a people into a state, we must at first never forget hereby that all such development is never in a position to

---

[116] [Lycurgus was the legendary law-giver of Sparta.]
[117] [Solon (6th c. B.C.) was an Athenian democratic statesman and legislator.]

CARL GUSTAV CARUS

become a fully finalized one; for, if already the Idea in and itself can never enter fully into reality, so also in mankind—in its mass of people ever renewing itself through births and in the endless diversity of all individual men, whereby the process of the development from the unconscious to self-consciousness necessarily likewise repeats itself anew endlessly—it is sufficiently guaranteed that the state never becomes a completely self-conscious and therewith an absolutely perfect whole. But the same factor on account of which that endless metamorphosis hinders, on the one hand, the absolute perfection of the state becomes, on the other hand, at the same time, the cause of continuing life and of the possibility of timely transformation of the same, because indeed now an unceasing activity and metamorphosis can be separated from the concept of the state, as an organism, as little as birth and death itself can.

Remark: Insofar as in all such things we are always aware of how perfectly even in the organism of the self-conscious state the concept of the unconscious racial life must constantly repeat itself in order to maintain, precisely through this, the vitality of the whole, the parallel between the state and a living creature necessarily becomes increasingly clearer; for, even in the latter, the principle of constant motion and continuous development devolves solely on the totally unconsciously operating individual plastic force, on a formative activity whose even momentary halt would always mean instant death but whose healthy unbroken continuation produces, alone and from the start, all the great life-metamorphoses of the whole. If therefore we have to differentiate between self-conscious political life and a constantly persisting ethnic life within it, then it will at the same time become clear, as a consequence of the above, how much the leader of the former has a reason to constantly pay close attention to the latter and how, indeed, all political life can be successfully directed only through a proper observation of the latter.

But now, if we could in the above with good reason compare the development of the state in many respects with the development of language, it follows now, at the same time, why the state too must gradually and involuntarily develop partly out of the unconscious of the race but partly also, just like language, has to be seen as an artifice of especially illuminated minds and, for this reason, cannot at all dispense with a deliberate cultivation of the personal mind to its perfection—a demand that is then comparable not only to a similar process in all linguistic development but also to the character of all hygiene as that through which our own physical organism can attain everywhere the true height and beauty of its nature.

I think further that just this pointer is required here to allow one to understand how much natural philosophy—because the complete foundation of doctrines of the organism is to be expected only from it—will always be especially suited to give a deeper explanation of the fundamental relations of the state and, therefore, little though it can be our task at present to go into all the subjects pertaining to this in greater detail, the enormous significance of the state for all higher cultivation of mankind obliges us to grant a more extensive scope to its observation and to pursue its division in detail a little further now and in such a way that we take into consideration—exactly as in the case of all other organisms—in it also, first its relation to the outside as well as the relation of its parts one to the other and to the whole and, then, the rise, operation, transformation, and decay of the same.

a. Of the external relations of the state

The closest external world of every state is the totality of mankind and then, specifically, other states and peoples, as well as external Nature.

Of course, one could first pose the question if all of mankind were not generally called to form a single state, though this remains so much more an unnatural thought in that the racial difference of the individual nations is so extraordinarily great and the development of the state presupposes always the, first, unconscious and, later, self-conscious striving of precisely one specific race for unity; consequently, every attempt to want to force the unification of all of mankind to a state without such a striving must lead to nothing but the juxtaposition of diverse elements, that is, therefore, to a completely unnatural and inorganic process and indeed will for that reason never be realized.

Remark: The necessary collapse of all attempts of bold conquerors to join together very different peoples lastingly and inwardly into a state is a fact through which history points to the truth of the above sentences. On the other hand, that all of mankind and all its major ethnic groups have, through internal development, become a real state and all these could and should unite in a large federal state is indeed a demand that philosophy must express as the highest goal of the development of mankind in general; whether, however, such an ideal will ever be reached may justly be doubted. In this context it must be observed also that already unifications of individual states and the incorporation of small states into larger ones has always been the occasion for endless conflicts between states and peoples. Of course, within a smaller scope many things are possible that must necessarily be considered impossible in a larger. Thus, for example, a surgeon can with special care transplant a piece of skin from one man to another, but, on the other hand, to set a foreign arm, or even a finger, onto another organism will always be impossible for him.

If it follows from the above that for the individual state, in its relation to other states and peoples, its most essential significance is only to contribute everywhere to the most perfect and always individual representation of the concept of the higher development of all of mankind, then it is obvious that this is never thinkable without a free and vital reciprocity. If it was realized earlier that no being, and generally nothing in the world, can exist fully isolated and, rather, that everything exists only insofar as it finds itself in a continuous reciprocity with the microcosm, then also, in individual cases, a fully self-enclosed state will always remain a nonsense and every attempt to realize something of this sort will be proved to be futile whereas, on the other hand, the flourishing of every state is established ever more certainly the more it finds itself, given a normal internal development, in a material and intellectual reciprocity with other divisions of mankind.

Remark: Even for these sentences the history of mankind offers copious examples; and the abstruse, and for the most part stunted, conditions in states like China and Japan—where, for such a long time, there prevailed an obstinate blockade against influences from other states—are excellent examples of this in that they recall the existence of plants or animals that have somehow been violently detached from external Nature. There is therefore hardly any aspect in which the wisdom or folly of a state government could, from the beginning, be demonstrated more than the degree of increase or reduction of material as well as intellectual reciprocity in relation to the outside world, since, on the one hand, blockades and, on the other, total absorption into it have always led to the worst results.

But not merely the conduct of the state towards other states appears to philosophical observation as the most important factor of life but also that towards other peoples not yet developed into states and towards the external Nature of the planet in general. As regards the former, here a similar relationship enters as that of the adult, intellectually mature man towards the immature child, and even hereby a remarkable organic factor is manifested; for, insofar as, on the one hand, the perfect political life draws in herewith certain immature elements and thereby the mission of universal development of mankind is advanced, it is also not excluded that precisely such elements for their part provide fresh blood to an already completed whole and protect it against stagnation and atrophy.

Not less significant is, in precisely this sense, the relationship of the state to external Nature. For it is this that, on the one hand, generally represents the sustaining soil of mankind and, on the other, also has to expect a manifold heightening of its character from an ordered state. Consequently, this includes everything that—in relation to the cultivation of the soil and the plant and animal culture dependent on it—was, and always will be, an important focus of attention of great legislators. For this reason also mankind capable of higher intellectual development flourishes only where soil, air, and water, climate, and food favour such processes through an indirect influence that promotes life; but also the nature of the land changes gradually in relation to the condition of mankind at any time—stunted either through deforestation, drying up of rivers, and bad cultivation in general, or it is raised through the opposites of all these factors; even the types of plant and animal are raised then and benefit in this rise their promoter.

If therefore we compare the state as a whole to a real human organism, the essential and characteristic organs of its assimilation lie only in its relation to the surrounding Nature, and, just as a man without the basis of a strong nourishment will not be capable of a truly significant activity in any direction, it is clear from the above that, quite similarly, the healthy relationship of the political life to external Nature must provide the first condition for the type of development of its men at any time.

But these observations naturally lead us now to dwell especially on:

b. The rise of a state

That in the same wonderful way that the personal spirit emerges from within mankind, so also the state from mankind and from within it, and that both processes further condition each other so precisely that only through the fact that an intellectual man develops does the state become possible and, again, only an ordered state conditions the developing mind—this is one of the deepest observations in which natural and intellectual philosophy constantly meet each other.

But, if it was already remarked earlier how, for just this gradual emergence of the state, the development of language provides a remarkable and illuminating analogy, it is to be acknowledged further that, if for the realization of the state generally the previous or contemporaneous development of language was at the same time the first condition, now as the second condition is demanded writing. For, in order to fix that which makes the state, law, a merely oral conception of it cannot suffice; law itself must be rescued somehow through its written codification from the realm of the constantly fluctuating, even quickly passing, individuality of man to a firmer, as it were abstract, existence if it should maintain itself as the foundation of the state, and already for this reason we may declare: no rise of a state without a written law, without a legal charter.

Remark: With this declaration we touch upon one of the most complex and far-reaching doctrines in the physiology and philosophy of the state, for which, moreover, the survey of concrete individual organisms remains of quite special importance. For one may maintain that the concept of the legal charter is related to the state exactly as that of the skeleton to the animal organism. Just as the latter truly obtains only through the skeleton a definite shape (whereby however It is presupposed that the skeleton itself preserves its total vitality and further development and does not itself decay and its ossification does not proceed too far into the soft tissues), the state too shapes itself everywhere only through the law, and yet the latter must never ossify absolutely and ossify the political life as a dead letter but, by constantly taking into account the transformation of the whole, it must—even if it in itself is a prohibiting, regulating, and retarding phenomenon—on the whole promote and enliven these transformations, which is a unification of two opposites which in practice was always one of the most disputed and hardest points in the conduct of all political life but ideally nevertheless is quite indisputably required.

It is now obvious that the realization of the written law cannot alone condition the entire rise of a state but that, at the same time, in that entity in which there was previously only a people and that should now develop into a state, the demand for an ordered condition and the need of law should not fail to become thoroughly animated, that, therefore, its consciousness become ever more vitally alert and, through this, the force be developed from the henceforth acknowledged law to allow itself to be completely intellectualized and to maintain it in such a way that individual members of the people that go against it from now on are brought to the observation of it either through kindness or strictness.

From all this then it follows directly that always, the more the concept of law arises and maintains itself in the people, so much more will also the Idea of the state as that of the highest development of mankind be realized and, then, so much more finely must the other life obligations be fulfilled in its operations and transformations, whereas the less the law penetrates the people and the more the latter are just forced to an observation of the law, the worse will it be also in the case of the fulfilment of the other tasks of political life. The difference between a slavish people and a free nation is to be clearly delineated only from this standpoint.

Remark: It is noteworthy that, in the most ancient monotheistic state of mankind, the Mosaic, already in the development of its people into a state, all emphasis is clearly placed on the law and the table of commandments, whereas, in the philosophy of polytheistic (Greek) states, on the other hand, in spite of their twelve centuries younger age and their excellence in the sciences, precisely this factor is placed less at the top. Aristotle, in his otherwise deep politics, proceeds here more according to genetics, that is, starting entirely from the organization of the family, in order to make political life comprehensible, whereas Plato moves closer to our subject and occupies himself first with the concept of justice, which obviously contains in itself, everywhere, that of law.

If the above has generally shown that there can be no talk of the rise of a state until it has attained not only a declaration but also the writing down of laws, so through a philosophical observation two more things of importance must be mentioned—first, that all laws establishing a state can be compared to the earlier-mentioned natural law regarding the equality of male and female births in that, just as the latter seemed not to exist for a few individual cases but manifested itself first only as a multiplicity, so also these laws emerge only when the consciousness of many is finally concentrated in a unity so that it now expresses clearly that which many previously felt only dimly as a necessity; secondly, however, that, if it is indeed a general truth that never and nowhere can absolute reason in itself enter into reality, no law too is to be expressed in such a perfect clarity that it does not in its application presuppose once again an intelligent mind that must judge to what extent any specific case is to be evaluated according to it.

From the above it further follows that the real realization of a state as an organic whole, both in its rise and in its continuation, could never forego the directing influence of higher individuals, so that not law alone but, at the same time, the personal mind must provide the condition that a state rises and exists. The manner in which this personality reveals himself can, further, be different every time. Even natural philosophy must consider it organically most appropriate when such a mind is embodied in one person as a judge, leader, prince, and only the lack of an adequate personality then justifies the substitution of a single person with the unity of many in the form of a council or senate (where, however, organic necessity every time presses towards the predominance of one personality). Modern times, however, have attained in constitutional monarchy a unification of the personality of the prince and the counselling majority of the classes and, even philosophically considered, this must therefore finally be called the relatively most perfect, that is, the one that is most suited to the needs of mankind.

The observation of the actions and transformations of the state we summarise in one concept as:

c. Political life

Just as, in the externally motionless and apparently quite tranquil body, there is an all-round movement, the juices circulate everywhere, the organs decompose and reconstruct themselves, and the nerves and muscle fibres vibrate, so also a state, even in peaceful external (political) relations, can never be imagined without the most lively action within, and there must be a constant activity and need, a rising and falling, decomposing and reconstructing in it, and, along with this activity, a persistent transformation must always be bound to it.

Further, one can observe even the individual branches of the internal political life according to the analogy of bodily functions and, through the right use of this analogy, as everywhere, gain in knowledge; and in this way we find then that—just as in the live body vegetative and animal functions are differentiated, the first of which is divided into nourishment and destruction, circulation and production, and as in the second are represented separately a sensitive and motor aspect, a materially supportive and a spiritually liberating one—so also the internal political life represents the twofold regions of material and ideal life, in which then on both sides a fourfold division can easily be distinguished in such a way that, in the first aspect, agriculture, military, trade, and education and, in the second, arts and manufacture, justice, as well as science and religion perfectly repeat that division.

The next application that is made possible by a survey of these analogous relations to the doctrine of the inner political life will always be the knowledge of the necessity of an inner reciprocal binding and intertwining of all individual state functions one to the other. It must doubtless become clear immediately that, just as those individual physical systems and organs are developed only from an original unity through continuous division, and each exists only through the commonalty of all, so also all those twice four regions of political life similarly only arise partly through an original division and partly can exist only through an internal mutual penetration with all others—a knowledge to which can be attached automatically a survey of the results that the history of states has yielded according to whether these truths were adhered to or not, from which important hints may be derived for the state leadership of the future and whither it has to direct mankind—

subjects whose details lie far from us here and at which we will have to cast a few glances only here and there.

But among the concepts that are the most significant and most often discussed in the context of political life are those of freedom and bondage, health and disease, and especially the first, which is indeed so closely tied to that of health.

But the true concept of that freedom—for which the noblest natures among the Greeks and Romans went to their death, whereas the same, on the other hand, was not less often the banner for the most ignorant and worst masses—is not more finely derived than from a view of a really healthy organism, where every system and every organ exercises its functions unhindered and with ease within the limits prescribed to it and, by seeming to be formed and to exist quite normally, that is, according to the norm, or the law prescribed to it, enjoys that which we call health, a condition that is announced to us too in our own body always through the feeling of perfect ease of living. What else therefore can the genuine freedom of political life too be called than a condition where each of the eight or, more correctly, nine spheres of political life fulfils its task unhindered and with ease and where no other limits are set to it than those that are determined for it by the welfare of the whole, in short, by freedom within the law. If therefore the history of states has enough examples to show where one-sided, arbitrary pressure and slave force destroyed entire states by at first bearing down on only individual limbs of the political life, on science and religion, or agriculture and manual work, or education, or trade, others are also not lacking that show how an Idea of freedom clearly and correctly conceived by a single illuminated mind—and at first only for a certain section of the political life—has been of the most enormous influence on the fortune of nations and on everything that one may call the welfare of a nation.

Remark: In this context perhaps hardly any example is more striking than the influence of that brilliant Scotsman Adam Smith[118] on the condition of material production and sales within the past century. The ever more widely progressed freedom of industry and trade and the circulation of money—which indeed may be compared in so many respects to the blood circulation of animal bodies—promoted thereby in the higher sense according to his principles, which were at that time still little understood, has confirmed his views multiple times and can offer rich opportunities for commentaries on the above sentences.

But political life appears as the reflection of an individual human life especially insofar as it is as insufficient for its concept (though it is generally fully sufficient for plants and animals) that it be a healthy one fully undisturbed in its inner actions but always in that whole, just as in each individual, will be demanded, at the same time, the fulfilment of a higher ideal goal, namely the realization of the full Idea of the divine in man, in beauty, love, and truth, and indeed through the development of his spiritual life as consciousness of the world, of self, and of God.

If therefore the philosophy of becoming had to acknowledge as a fine and indispensable transition that already in the higher organisms of plants and animals a perfectibility was revealed through the influence of human intelligence that can in no way be content with a simply healthy life but strives to transform this life itself always according to a higher Idea, so for the highest circle of life on earth the natural condition alone remains completely insufficient, so that then now even for the state a merely affluent existence through lively internal transactions and external enjoyment cannot simply satisfy in the case of higher demands but

---

[118]   See the fine new French edition of his works: *Recherches sur la nature et les causes de la richesse des nations*, 3 vols, Paris, 1859.

even from it is necessarily demanded an internal cultivation according to the above-mentioned higher goals.

That therefore which was fulfilled in the natural prototypes of the state—still fully unconsciously—as in the state of bees—love for otherwise helpless brood, the beauty in the tectonic of cell structures, and the true regularity in the conduct of the whole— that should now (as is clearly demonstrated now, in a logical manner, also through natural philosophy) be consciously cultivated in the political state of men, indeed in such a way that all those individual branches of the material as well as ideal political life are now inwardly and outwardly informed increasingly by the three Ideas inborn in mankind, of beauty, love, and truth, a task however that would be impossible to fulfil if the second demand were not satisfied at the same time that requires that the state's consciousness of the world and of the self be crowned most excellently through its consciousness of God.

Indeed, one may therefore declare that in these two demands are contained and specified the essential goals and measures for all internal actions and transformations of the political life and, since now in all of this one is to start from the fact that within such a life every activity and form must in time unceasingly somehow become something else, because indeed the concept of no life can be separated from that of the constant death and renewal, so now it must indisputably be called the ideal of such an unceasingly progressing metamorphosis if even the newly born entity constantly grasps at those goals more firmly and more completely than that which perished could—with which, to be sure, reality is always little able to agree because it will always remain a higher law that reason must be moderated in everything by an addition of a certain irrationalism in order to be able to be realized finally even just to a certain degree.

CHAPTER II

Remark: It would go far beyond the aim and scope of the present observations if I wished to explain in detail now the general statements offered above with facts and proofs from history. But nobody who has given himself the trouble to absorb the deep inner basis of something so universally true will neither be in a position to underestimate the natural basis of the same nor to ignore the many examples of historical processes that emerge daily. For we see from the beginning that states which got bogged down in stifling exclusiveness and sluggishness soon collapsed as necessarily as those that lacked self-consciousness and self-mastery to such an extent that lawlessness and insolence prevailed everywhere whereas, in contrast, others, through the dedication of a pure God-consciousness, often attained greater stability and dignity of existence, a truth that is already announced by the fact that only in the Christian era one can generally speak of a perfect cultivation of a political life developing through legalistic freedom, a cultivation that—even if it has not by far reached its own ideal—precedes all that which was earlier possible here and there in pagan states through the coincidence of favourable circumstances, and which would indeed have progressed further if the still lawless condition of the states among themselves had not pressed on each individual one of them in such a way that the immoderately increasing expansion of the military had to condition a disturbance of the free development of all other political functions and therewith the actual moral development of the entire political life was faced with insuperable obstacles.

Two other factors finally remain of special importance in a philosophical context for the doctrine of political life and these are: partly, the constant influence of the unconscious of the people or of the nation on the process of the further development of the whole, and, partly, the significance of the history of the state for its own further development.

As regards the former, even where one spoke of the ever newly emerging and constantly renewing human mass of a state, the fact is already pointed out that is important: that a people as a whole can never really mature, that is, arrive at a legal consciousness, and precisely for this reason must also retain something of that which we define in the animal world as presentiment or instinct, and which the ancients already called the *vox dei*,[119] which, however, deserves such a name only in a very general sense; for even here, unlike among animals, if one speaks of a true and completely unconscious mass, the actual wisdom of the unconscious can never manifest itself with such clarity as there, and remains instead far more momentary and local, often subject to the greatest errors. However, the instinct of the peoples in history has always occupied itself with the most important things and remains also, finally, the real fundamental cause by which the quiet motion of the nations, proceeding through centuries and millennia, is chiefly conditioned.

But if it is indeed finally always this unconscious by which the history of peoples and states is made, on the other hand it is history itself—as the present realization of those movements—that is once again that by which this unconscious increasingly attains consciousness and whereby finally that progress from world-consciousness to self- and God-consciousness of the peoples—which provides the true measure of the cultural level—is chiefly, indeed solely, manifested.

Such a becoming increasingly conscious of itself, such a survey of its own development therefrom, these are now chiefly that through which the state in mankind will always differentiate itself from the prototypes of the same in the animal world to such an extent that, if the latter are repeated in eternal monotony always

---

119   [Voice of God.]

only as themselves, the former must everywhere and at all times be an individualized phenomenon that becomes new every time.

d. The passing of a state

Even here many things are presented that are noteworthy for physiological-philosophical observation, for it is represented, first of all, that generally the inevitable necessity of a predestined death does not take place as in the case of individual real organisms. A state that recognizes its significance, neither hinders nor disregards the inner renewal and life-metamorphosis that must infuse every living thing, can last for endless ages and even inspire and strengthen itself through an ever-widening survey of its history. That this goal is in reality seldom reached, and only with difficulty, is due to two reasons—that is, states die particularly of disease or through external violence.

For the first, there lies, first of all, an essential cause, and one that is hard to avoid, in its own unceasing internal productivity and the overpopulation resulting from that. If indeed it cannot be denied at all that all truly higher humanity (language, the mind) only emerges through a multiplicity of men, precisely this multiplicity again becomes—even though it, on the one hand, conditions the daylight of the intellect—on the other hand, the occasion for the night of the intellect; for, naturally, the more individuals are crowded together, the more do diseases, crime, luxury, and misery develop in such a way that finally thereby, in many respects, the unity of the political life itself collapses.

However, the actual unconscious of the peoples has always, on the presentiment of such a danger, resorted to the same means that can be observed with equal clarity in the natural state of many animals; there arose then in most cases in the state the instinct to emigration, and in this way, in a wonderfully harmonious manner, the flight from misery became hundreds of times the means of the natural spread of mankind over the earth—an inner wisdom of that unconscious, which is perhaps a hint that recommends as a goal, even to the conscious influence of the leaders of the state, the serious matter of orderly migrations of peoples.

More seldom does natural devastation—a devastation that tends to be occasioned only by natural events, terrestrial revolutions, floods, droughts, and epidemics, or through violence suffered in destructive wars—appear as a cause of the sickening of states that can also, however, cause them to die. However, though we recall violence in this second cause of the downfall of a state, we must at the same time mention it as significant for the state—as the real peak of mankind—what power of resistance it can mostly exercise against all such destructive influences so long as it remains completely healthy in itself. The characteristic tenacity and the constant reestablishment of every living being, which has already been noticed many times above in the observation of real organisms, and which tends to be preserved thousands of times even in the plant and animal world, is not only similarly characteristic to a high degree of the physical and intellectual organism of man, but it has been proved often most clearly in history since the Persian Wars of the Greeks and similar events, when even the smallest state—so long as it remained healthy and vital—was often combated in vain by the most powerful ones and was in a position to maintain its individuality in the greatest attacks of this sort, so that then here too everything perfectly comes together to restore the characteristic organic nature of that whole that we call a state.

Conclusion

But these observations of ours should not extend further, since it would be sufficient to show, in general as well as in detail, how everything that develops—no matter how indefinitely manifold, how arbitrary, and often how apparently lawless its manifestation appears—adheres everywhere and completely to eternal laws, and how everything unequal and unstable in that monstrous phenomenon that we conjure up with the term nature nevertheless remains in its innermost being constantly regulated by Idea—the primordial image of every being in God. For, just as we generally started from the fact that every philosophy must as certainly always silently presuppose God as every circle necessarily must its centre, so too the entire mode of our observations could only continuously provide us with proofs that, in the uranic as well as in the telluric and epitelluric, in formation as well as in movement, eternal divine laws operate everywhere with iron necessity—a necessity that rises to the freedom of self-consciousness only when, in the highest aethereal action, that is, in innervation, a reflection of the divine itself emerges even in the form of mind, a reflection whose own perfection, however, is once again attained only through the fact that it sacrifices its own freedom to the universal laws, or rather that it recognizes the same as innate in its own being, and that from then onwards it acts only in accord with them and in this way returns to God in an actual sense.

So I wish here to point further only to how this thought process, which we see here emerge with so much precision from the principles of natural philosophy and confirmed in all its individual observations, obviously forms, at the same time, the essential core of all mysteries in which man, driven by his deepest feelings always to the original source of his being, has always found, and will continue to find, his highest satisfaction. The task of a pure intellectual philosophy must then necessarily remain to pursue exhaustively that which could be expressed here only in a preparatory and suggestive manner in all its applications and determinations—a task whose fulfilment is certainly to be expected all the more when a healthy and genuine natural philosophy has prepared the way to it everywhere in the right direction.